We
(On Friendship)

Scott Abbott & Žarko Radaković

We (On Friendship)
Copyright © 2022 by Scott Abbott

All rights reserved. Printed in the United States of America. No part of this book may be used or reproduced in any manner whatsoever without written permission except in the case of brief quotations embodied in critical articles or reviews.

For information contact
Elik Press
962 E. Lowell Ave.
Salt Lake City, UT 84102

Cover design: D Christian Harrison
Book design: Deb Thornton

www.elikpress.com
ISBN-978-0-9818567-9-7

Contents

Scott Abbott: On Friendship

    1 Žarko Radaković: Approximately   3

    2 An Amicable Correspondence   32

    3 A Friendly Epilogue   71

Žarko Radaković: We

    1 Friends   75

    2 Secret of the Absent Friend   103

    3 Accomplices (Witnesses)   113

Afterwords and Portraits

    Alex Caldiero: Regarding WE   129

    Nina Pops: Portraits   131

About the Authors   133

Acknowledgements   135

On Friendship

Scott Abbott

For Alex Caldiero

1

Žarko Radaković
Approximately

Žarko transports us to a South Sea island and asks what I'm writing. Your biography, I answer. He outfits me with a cigar. Takes me to hear John Zorn. Bathes me with Monique.

Although a reader may be excused for supposing his account a "figment of the imagination," let me assure you that every word Žarko Radaković has written is true. As St. Nietzsche taught us in his extra-moral treatise, truth is a mobile army of metaphors.

Žarko watches me write, writes about watching me write. He assumes I'm working on his biography. That's impossible here, at this table on the South Sea island he has imagined. The closest I have come to an island in the Pacific Ocean was by proxy. Bob Abbott, my young father-to-be, navigated a B-29 bomber from the islands of Tinian and Iwo Jima to pound the hell out of Japan. Žarko's father Mirko Radaković fought Nazis in Yugoslavia during that same war. Both men returned home alive, courted and married our mothers, Ljubica Pantic and Janice Hilton, and we were born in 1947 and 1949, respectively.

I decide to move us from Žarko's fantasy island to my house in Utah. Embraced by Wasatch Mountains and overlooking the shallow lake nestled in Utah Valley, I can approximate Žarko's life in a familiar setting. At the end of novel *Pogled* (The View), Žarko's narrator asks: "Who are we 'here'?" Who is Žarko? I will ask. Who is he "here," in my space, in my time?

Žarko's friend David Albahari reminds me that biography is approximate at best: "I cannot even attempt to reconstruct his life. Every biography is as futile at laying claim to truth as is an autobiography. One witness is not enough, and the statements of two witnesses are never identical."

My brother John died of AIDS-related causes in 1991 and for twenty-five years I wrote about him, fragments I came to think of as fraternal meditations. I found I could not write about John without writing about myself. *Immortal for Quite Some Time* was finally published in 2016. This approximate biography of my dear friend Žarko Radaković, drawn from notes beginning in 1984 when I made his acquaintance in Tübingen, Germany, will be a sequel of sorts to *Immortal for Quite Some Time*.

Why did I write about my brother? Why am I writing about Žarko? Nobel Prize awardee Ivo Andrić offers one answer to those questions:

> He was looking for a compassionate fellow spirit who would be willing to listen and would have an endless capacity for understanding, to whom he might talk openly and receive lucid and honest answers to all questions. In this dialogue he might then, as in a mirror, see himself for the first time as he really was and learn the true value of his work and determine, without ambiguity, his own position in the world.

Žarko and I are polar opposites with much in common. While my country's Un-American Activities Committee was investigating Hollywood screenwriters and directors as suspected Communists, Žarko's father was beginning his career as a post-war Communist functionary in a country where Communist Partisans were heroes of the new Republic.

Žarko's mother grew up in a village in the mountains of Fruska Gora where her father was a prosperous farmer. My mother grew up in Denver, Colorado, where her father was an insurance salesman. Žarko's father was from Surčin, near Belgrade, where his father was a well-to-do farmer. My father grew up in the small town of Windsor, Colorado, where his father was a well-to-do farmer. My father had five palomino horses. The number of Žarko's father's palomino horses has not been determined to my satisfaction.

Žarko's young mother leans back in a light dress the colors of which the black-and-white photo don't reveal. She holds her bigheaded little boy high against her chest. Shirtless, the bald savant looks down at his mother, gestures with his big right hand. Her downturned head, closed eyes, and suppressed grin suggest that she has heard this lecture before. After reading Žarko's novel *Tübingen* she had no grin to suppress. If you write another book like this, she said, you will end up in an asylum. When my mother read *Wild Rides and Wildflowers: Philosophy and Botany with Bikes*, the abundant profanity made her worry I would end up in Hell.

Long-legged Žarko, 7 or 8 years old, sits astride a small wooden horse. He looks like anything but a cowboy: short pants, knee socks, sandals, a knee-length overcoat, and a beret. What will become of this little boy with his enigmatic smile?

The same boy, maybe a year younger or perhaps a year older, sits on a bench between his father and a family friend. All three wear overcoats and hats. Žarko's father sports a fedora, the other man a cap with a short bill, Žarko what looks like a baseball cap. The two men watch a soccer game on a local field. Žarko has turned to the camera, his outsized ears as avid as his lively eyes. Big hands hang from his overcoat sleeves, already hungry for a pen.

Tiny, dark-haired Milica gazes up at her young father. His long-fingered hand stretched around her back holds her securely. Is she fascinated by Žarko's moustache? By his sweet gaze looking down at her? Olga and I were young, Žarko says, and very much in love.

Žarko spent a year doing compulsory military service. One photo shows a lean, short-haired young man in a uniform shirt. A mustache droops over his full-lipped mouth, serious eyes fixed on the camera. At about that same time I was in Germany doing semi-compulsory Mormon missionary work. I narrowly avoided the draft for the Viet Nam War. I can't imagine Žarko and myself as killers. A clear failure of imagination.

Did you ever play an instrument other than a gun? I ask Žarko, who has set down his notebook and pen to gaze out over a valley shimmering in the hot afternoon sun.

I was listening to the crickets in your oak brush, he says. And now you ask me about music. My parents gave me an old piano when I was young. I had perfect pitch, they said, and they sent me to music school. Some years later, I fell in love with my brother Miloje's piano teacher at the same school. She was pretty, a pianist, and she was my first love, my first woman. I listened to classical music with her, especially Bach, her favorite. When I was only 14, before my "music teacher," local jazz musicians practiced on our piano, a rarity in the neighborhood. One pianist was the younger brother of a trumpet player who went to New York and played with Woody Herman. He and I sometimes played the blues together, I with my left hand, he with his right. It was his fault I left music school. He took me to performances in Belgrade by musicians from the Newport Jazz Festival. I heard them all live, those great musicians from the 60s. A piece of luck. That's the way it was.

Žarko heard Louis Armstrong, Ella Fitzgerald, MJQ, Art Farmer, Roland Kirk, Oskar Peterson, Dave Brubeck, and Miles Davis. Music invented by descendants of slaves in New Orleans and refined in Chicago, Kansas City, New York City, and Los Angeles, American music performed in Communist Belgrade by black musicians discriminated against in their own country. Ella Fitzgerald was refused lodging in Salt Lake City's Hotel Utah—not far north from where we are sitting. Contralto Marion Anderson was allowed to stay there, but only if she used the freight elevator.

I grew up in an isolated farming town in northwestern New Mexico where the musical highlight was a visiting Australian boys choir singing "Waltzing Matilda" to a small audience at the Elk's Club. I took piano lessons from a nice old lady who agreed, after my enthusiastic but uninspired performance of Beethoven's "Für Elise," that there was no real reason for me to continue. As for jazz, citizens of our little town saw civil rights activists and radical jazz musicians like Charles Mingus and Billie Holiday as enemies of the free and open democracy we cherished.

Belgrade, Žarko says, his finger marking a page in his re-opened notebook, Belgrade was a lively, open city, a city between cultures, between East and West. It was nowhere. Or exactly in the center. A magnet for artists of many kinds, including jazz musicians. These days I listen to a lot of Baroque music, because of Anne.

You got lucky with Anne, I say. You married after 23 years together and said you loved her more than you ever had.

I still feel that way, Žarko says.

We were talking about music.

Yes, we were. When I hear jazz I'm at home, a child again. Writing *A Book about Music* with David Albahari was one of the most beautiful experiences of my life as a writer.

Writing the books *Repetitions* and *Vampires & A Reasonable Dictionary* with Žarko was life changing for me. Two distinct voices, one American, one European, improvising on the tune "Peter Handke," on the tune "travel," on the tune "the American West," on the tune

"Yugoslavia," on the tune "destruction of Yugoslavia at the hands of nationalist assholes," on the tune "American vampires," on the tune "friendship." During the night drive through Germany at the end of the trip described in *Repetitions*, Louis Armstrong and Ella Fitzgerald danced cheek to cheek on the radio, an inspiration for our parallel, repetitive, radically different responses to what we had just experienced in Austria and Slovenia . . . and later for our thoughts about shared experiences in Utah and along the Drina River.

Sitting on my deck, Žarko alternately overlooks the mountain-rimmed valley and writes in his notebook. For years he favored Waterman fountain pens. Now he writes with a stylish Caran d'Ache. I buy my pens twelve-for-$10.

Žarko experimented with performance artists Era and Marina Abramović in Belgrade while I read French and Russian novels in Farmington, New Mexico, . . . and, I have to admit, fat novels by the Russian-American, virulently anti-Communist and insanely capitalist Ayn Rand. I liked the sex scenes.

Were you ever a Communist? I ask.

Only an American would ask that question, Žarko answers. In the Kingdom of Yugoslavia, my maternal grandfather was a rich farmer with 150 hectares of land. The Communists appropriated the land and he became a modest farmer. And he was fine with that. Three of his sons fought for the Resistance in the war, one of them died, all three were Communists. Communists were heroes in the war, the country a product of our version of Communism. In school we learned to be patriots: "small country yet independent and courageous." My father was a Communist at work but not at home. Otherwise I would not be the person I am. 1968 was a kind of collective maturation for us—as it was with activists in Germany, in France, and possibly in the United States. The Germans had to deal with the fact that their parents had been Nazis. We knew there were victims of Communism; we weren't naïve. I introduced you once to a poet who was jailed for four months for comparing Tito to a bear—a big boost to his standing as a poet. When I visited you in the USA for the first time, I applied for a visa and had to answer the question whether I had ever been a member of the Communist Party. If I had answered "yes," it's possible I would have been denied a visa. What kind of democracy is that?

Žarko's gaze jumps from Utah Lake to the gathering clouds above Mt. Timpanogos and then to the alfalfa field several hundred feet below us. His mind wears seven-league boots. My mind jumps from boots to my brother's apartment after his death. John had cut out the shapes of his feet from a cardboard box to line his work shoes. I framed the cardboard and backed the holes with Miroslav Mandić's drawings of feathery, grassy, and pebbly feet, traces of his poetic pilgrimage from Yugoslavia to Hölderlin's grave in Tübingen.

Was Mandić part of the group with Era and you in Belgrade?

No, Žarko answers. Mandić was from Novi Sad, one of a group of poets who worked conceptually. They still see themselves as the origin of conceptualism in Yugoslavia. That's absurd. We were all in the same boat: a boat that sank, as is well known. In Belgrade we were all visual artists, except for me, although I did that one piece of concrete poetry you have seen in my flat: "Medex." It was for our performance #1, 1971, at the Belgrade International Theater Festival.

I visualize the extended hexagon fashioned by Žarko's strategically typed medmedmedmedmed. At the top two sharp pointed swarms of "z"s enter or leave the literal hive.

Era wrote the performance piece called "Medex," Žarko says. We lived together in a creative commune in apartment 10 b in Ljube Didića street. Three of us had studied literature together: Miodrag Vuković, one of the greatest Serbian-Montenegrin writers of my generation—he and I wrote some poems together; Nebojša Janković, now a journalist in Canada; and I. Era Milivojević joined us. He was already an artist of note, together with Marina Abramović who went on to stardom in New York. The title "Medex" came from a Yugoslavian company that produced honey and honey products. Their motto was "good and healthy products." The four of us were bees.

That photo of the four of you in striped sweaters lying on your stomachs, head to bushy head? Your mouths busy producing honey?

Exactly. There was also a queen bee, a sexy woman Era chased across the stage. And a good-hearted beekeeper along with two noisemakers. My brother Miloje tortured a metal plate to make a terrific noise.

Why bees?

They were archaic, natural, mythical—exactly the values we felt were being threatened. Honey. Remarkable stuff. Bees. Good creatures. I wrote a poem about insects called "Events in a Dark Chamber." And so on. Era was an enormous influence on me, turned me from literature to conceptual art.

The cover of Žarko's book *Era* presents Era with his bare limbs grotesquely constricted by rubber bands during a 1973 performance called "Turtle." Žarko stands in the photo as well, his back to the camera, wearing black pants, a long-sleeved white shirt, and shoulder-length hair bound by a strip of cloth. A portable record player squats on the floor between him and Era.

I can't read the book *Era*. I can't read any of Žarko's books except the two we wrote together.

With the help of my little dictionary/rečnik, described in detail in "A Reasonable Dictionary," I decipher the epigraph for *Era*, a quotation from T. S. Eliot's *Four Quartets*: "Time present and time past / Are both perhaps present in time future." Žarko signed the book with a related message: "For my friend Scott, words from the times that were, perhaps, only a dream." A dream that may be present in time future, I think, in the form of our books, in the form of our children and grandchildren. When I told Žarko's mother I had seven children, she said that Žarko had given her only a single grandchild, "lazy man that he is." I defended my friend: Žarko has more books than I have children. And you have to admit, Milica is a wonderful granddaughter. That's true, she said. That's certainly true.

I'm headed inside to get us something to drink, but first I ask if Era liked music.

Era and I listened mostly to Bob Dylan, Žarko answers. As you know, for a long time my English consisted of phrases from Dylan's songs.

You could have done worse.

Žarko turns his head from the valley to the mountains east of us, watches a white, gibbous moon rise from behind Santaquin Peak, notes his responses with his beautiful pen.

I get beer from the refrigerator and while inside thumb through my rečnik. I'm surprised to find no entry for "žarko." In his *A Journey to the Rivers*, Peter Handke says the name means "fiery." But there is no "žarko" in my dictionary. I look up my own name as it appears on the cover of our second book: "Skot": "Beast, vermin." My parents should have been more careful. I flip again through the "z" section and discover that "z" is followed by a set of words that begin with "ž." Serbo-Croatian works with more than 26 letters. Diacritical marks like the haček are placed over a letter to alter pronunciation: Ž, ž, Š, š, Č, č, ć, and đ.

Back on the deck, a bottle of Utah pilsner in each hand, I witness a metamorphosis. Bulging muscles fill out Žarko's tight-fitting black costume. A leather ammunition belt loaded with lethal diacritical marks crisscrosses his powerful chest. A silver-plated, rhodium-coated Varius Caran d'Ache fountain pen topped with a silver skull and tightly bound in leather stands erect in a holster on one hip. On the opposite hip, a black notebook, its pages loosened with desire, rests snug in a second holster. Diacritical Man.

Serbo-Croatian, especially since the disintegration of the Federal Republic, is confusing for American publishers. In a review of English translations of two books by David Albahari, I explained that the language once spoken on the "Highway of Brotherhood and Unity" that connected Zagreb and Belgrade was officially Serbo-Croatian, a unified and unifying language. Books translated into English while the highway still acted as a hyphen between the two cities, books like Ivo Andrić's *The Bridge on the Drina*, were "translated from the Serbo-Croat." But since the brutal wars of the 1990s that separated the republic into sovereign states and that shattered multicultural Yugoslav identities forged over seven decades, American publishers have struggled with how to designate the language of books coming out of the former Yugoslavia. The copyright page of Ranko Marinković's *Cyclops* (Yale, 2010), for instance, vacillates between two options: "originally published in Serbo-Croatian" and "originally published in Croatian by Prosveta, Beograd, 1965, former Yugoslavia." The idea of a book in Croatian published in Serbian Belgrade is as odd as the Dalkey Archive's 2012 edition of Danilo Kiš's *Psalm 44* that claims the book was "originally published in Serbian by Globus" in the Croatian capital Zagreb. Žarko still refers to his language as Serbo-Croatian. He is a gentle Serb with friends and collaborators in Slovenia, Montenegro, Croatia, Bosnia-Herzegovina, Macedonia, and Kosovo.

A gentle man whose name means fiery.

When the United States and NATO were bombing Belgrade in 1999, a cruise missile struck a building 400 meters from Žarko's mother's apartment. That same year Bill Clinton visited Cologne. I want to assassinate him, Žarko told me. Bill Clinton arrived and with a malapropism reproduced in giant, front-page letters the next morning, told the citizens of Köln: "Ich bin ein Kölsch." Mollified by the gaffe, Žarko decided against assassination.

Gospodin Fiery and Mister Vermin had a bitter dispute when Gospodin Fiery issued a stern corrective lecture in response to Mister Vermin's review of David Albahari's two books. Angry Mr. Vermin told the fiery critic he was clueless when it came to American readers, that he didn't read English that well anyway, and that he should keep his lectures to himself. Gentle Gospodin Fiery asked if the friendship was definitively over. Mister Repentant Vermin replied that this friendship would never die.

Žarko and I communicate in German, a second language for us both. We are, then, somewhat reduced versions of ourselves in the language we share. Our friend, the poet Alex Caldiero, doesn't count German among his languages (Sicilian, Italian, French, Spanish, and English). Alex sends Žarko his books and Žarko returns the favor. Alex responded to the gift of Žarko's novel *Kafana* with a claim to have read it:

> Dear Zarko,
> hope this letter finds you well. Want not only to thank you for the book you gave me via Scott . . . but to tell you that it had a profound effect on me. This is a lot, considering the fact that it is written in a language I do not understand. After I read about 20 pages out-loud, i began to hear your voice and, continuing to lissen to what i was reading, i stopped reading and began to write. . . . Is it translation? Is it original writing? Is it a genre of language all its own? No matter. It is my response and deeply held conviction that the field of language is vaster than our tongues can know. . . . There is no book that we cannot read. There is no language that we cannot understand.
> I send you a hug,
> as ever your friend and brother,
> Alex

Words, for Alex, are living beings. They are for me as well, although not as literally as for Alex. Late last year I lay in bed thinking about Žarko's and Albahari's *Book about Music*. I thought about Svetislav Basara's *Fama o biciklistima*, which I had just read in translation: *The Cyclist Conspiracy*. I was awake because Dubravka Ugrešić and Milorad Pavić and Slavenka Drakulić and Dragan Velikić and Zoran Živković and Danilo Kiš and Aleksandar Tišma and Ismet Prcic and Miljenko Jergović and Dragan Aleksić and Ranko Marinković and Drago Jančar and Boris Pahor and Vitomil Zupan and Aleksandar Hemon and Milcho Manchevski and Goran Radovanović and a dozen other Serbo-Croatian-Bosnian-Montenegrin-Macedonian-Slovenian wizards mocked me from the titles of their books and films. I counted critical but unfamiliar diacritical marks in the names and titles until I

We

found myself floating down the Drina River toward the Višegrad bridge where Ivo Andrić stood waiting for me. We entered a large plane and after it took off I was required to take over the controls. The first slight pressure against the stick made the plane pitch toward the ground. We will all die, I thought. I experimented with the stick while watching out a side window for glimpses of the ground to guide me. Eventually the fuel gage reached empty and I landed the big plane on the short dark runway of a tiny airport. I needed to refuel but couldn't make sense of the hose connections on what I took to be the pump. A man approached and said he would fill up the fuel tanks if I would go in and sign the proper papers. I knew that was impossible; I was not the authorized pilot. Ivo Andrić spoke to the man at the pump and said he would sign the papers himself. Did Andrić know I was an American? Wouldn't that be problematic? We had just bombed Belgrade. The plane was eventually fueled up, but I couldn't make out the runway in the darkness. Telephone poles and a high building and thick trees crowded into what should be open space. I walked along tracks through the trees, tracks that looked like they had been made by airplanes. If I disassembled the plane, I thought, it too could be pushed along this trail. I emerged from the trees and watched a plane take off from the little field. It lifted off the ground at the last second and then pulled straight up, just missing a tall building. I wondered whether I could make the large plane do that. Back in the pilot's seat, I tried to calculate the necessary speed. I checked the wind direction. I didn't know the weight of the plane. Could the passengers throw out their luggage? What if they dispensed with all diacritical marks?

When Žarko and Anne visited me in Utah, we drove through southern Utah, New Mexico, and Arizona. One night we stayed in a motel on Route 66 in Gallup, New Mexico, owned by a man from Pakistan and tucked into a corner of the Navajo Reservation. The next morning, we went to a weekend flea market just outside of town: Navahos trading and selling everything from turquoise-and-silver jewelry to car parts to native medicines to mutton stew. Anne flitted excitedly from pickup to pickup and rushed back to announce: Scott, we're the only Americans here!

In 1991 I received a postcard from Žarko: Lieber Scott, aus der Welt, die es vielleicht nicht mehr gibt. Dein Freund, Žarko (Dear Scott, from the world that perhaps no longer exists, your friend, Žarko). Yugoslavia's civil war. The postmark was Cologne, where I had visited him that spring. One night we saw Amos Poe's 1977 film *The*

Foreigner. A German comes to New York for some indeterminate business. He is attacked in front of the United Nations building, then shot in Battery Park with the Statue of Liberty looming in the background. In its root sense, the German word for misery, *Elend (eli-lenti)*, means "out, away from one's country."

In the early 1990s, Žarko spoke to students and faculty at my university about himself, about his work, and about his country.

> Approximately fifteen years ago I left my country. Back then, in 1978, it called itself the Socialist Federal Republic of Yugoslavia. . . . I didn't have the least suspicion that in fifteen years, that is, now, my country would no longer exist. . . .
>
> My ancestors were Serbian refuges. After the defeat on the Kosovo Polje, the Field of Blackbirds, they served as guards on the southern borders in the Dalmatian, Croatian, and what was then Austro-Hungarian hinterland. From there they moved as nomads to the fertile and sparsely inhabited plains of Pannonia, to Vojvodina between Hungary and Romania. Several centuries later I was born there. I grew up in Belgrade. And since the late seventies I have lived in Germany. —
>
> Haven't I always had something of the nomadic spirit of my ancestors in me? Haven't I shunned every uniformity and every emphasis on a center? To be Serbian and not simultaneously some second or third thing on this always complex (unintelligible) Balkan peninsula—that seems to me today an impossible thought. . . .
>
> Now the country has split into warring ethnic groups. In Yugoslavia there remain nothing but memories of free movement.

My friendships with Žarko, who left Yugoslavia for Germany, and with Alex, who left Sicily at the age of nine to settle in Brooklyn with his family, reward me with relationships in which I too am a foreigner.

As an immigrant, Žarko went to work for an arm of the German government. Peter Handke describes the vagaries of Žarko's employment in his *Journey to the Rivers*:

> Žarko Radaković, translator of several of my things into Serbian and à ses heures, as it is put so well in French, "in his

hours," himself a writer; though professionally, after studying in Belgrade and then for a long time in Tübingen, he became a translator and reader of German-language newspaper articles for the Balkan-directed division of Deutsche Welle radio—where, in a not infrequent conflict between being Serbian and having to speak against Serbia (as in the tendentious, never even faintly "pro-Serbian" fusillades of the *Frankfurter Allgemeine Zeitung*), he is a faithful translator, although he reads sometimes with a faltering voice.

Working in the tall tower in Cologne for a foreign bureaucracy was excruciating. The novel *Pogled* (The View), Žarko tells me, is a testament of that tortured existence.

Žarko leaves the deck and goes into my study to write an email to his publisher. I can hear his fingers striking the keyboard with rapid rhythmic thumps. Silence. Then another flurry. It dawns on me suddenly: he's typing Serbian sentences! On my keyboard!

Žarko's *Emigracia* (Emigration) and *Strah od Emigracije* (Fear of Emigration) are about leaving home. His first novel, *Tübingen*, is set in the university town where he and his wife Zorica Papadopolos, a theoretical physicist, first settled.

I met Žarko in Tübingen. I was there to write about the Freemasonic structure of Goethe's *Wilhelm Meisters Wanderjahre* (Journeyman Years). At night I worked on scraps of my own novel called "Tübingen." The manuscript still lurks on a shelf, abandoned to write the scholarly book about Freemasonry and the German novel. Žarko was writing a literary-critical dissertation in the German Department at the University of Tübingen. At least twice he has given me the title of the dissertation, a study inspired by Wolfgang Iser's reception theory, a title so abstract that I fall asleep trying to remember it. The dissertation may well have been brilliant and I can certainly imagine Žarko as a genial professor of Germanistik in the Philosophical Faculty of the University of Belgrade. He became a writer instead, inspired by two remarkable men.

In 1984, Žarko met Julije Knifer, a painter from Zagreb who had a studio in Tübingen. Žarko's "first film," a documentary about his interactions with Knifer, begins with Zorca washing dishes in their apartment. The camera shifts to several big trucks at the office of a construction firm, then pans up to a single window under a gable. Returning to ground level, the camera enters the front door. A quick glance into the doorkeeper's room, back into the hall, around corners, up stairs, past a sign announcing high voltage, and then a coffee machine. Up more stairs, down more halls, a kitchen for the workers. Everything empty and silent except for the sound of the camera's zoom. A door. A knock. Julije Knifer opens the door. The camera scans a dozen large canvases: meanders, black on white, white on black. The film continues, Žarko says, for seven hours.

Žarko showed me clips of the film in 1991 in his and Anne's apartment on Cologne's narrow little Herthastraße. The apartment felt to me like the heart of creative Cologne. We worked in adjoining rooms. One morning Žarko came into the living room where I was bent over my notebook and began looking through a cupboard. I once did an interview with an Albanian terrorist, he said. I need that now for my crime novel.

The mountain to the east is golden in the late-afternoon sun. Žarko has returned to the deck and, offering him wine and cheese, I ask him about Knifer. His name has an ominous look in English.

It *is* an English name, Žarko replies. His great-grandfather was an English Jew, a butcher and knife sharpener. Thus Knifer. In Tübingen I spent weeks watching him paint his black-and-white meanders. First the white paint on the canvas. Then another white coat and another and another. Julije said it made him anxious to think of the first black marks and so he would add another coat of white. And another. Or he painted the canvas black and then black again and again before he added the white. Watching Knifer reminded me that I had once been an artist and I began my "slow return home." Germanistik, secondary analysis—I still admire that—but I turned to primary production. As you know, I wrote my book *Knifer* to keep Julije's work alive in my own.

Žarko's book includes a long interview with Knifer, photos of Knifer at work, and photos of several of his murals. Fanciful captions under the photos of Knifer's geometrical meanders identify the vertical black lines as people: Žarko and his brother Miloje in a Zemun restaurant, 1960; Swiss writer Jürg Beler, Žarko, and I in Tübingen, 1979; Žarko and Zorca in Tübingen, 1979. All books are also about their authors.

I bring a notebook from the study to refresh my memory of our visit with Knifer in Paris. December 9, 1995. The high-ceilinged apartment was animated by a small, thin, unshaven man with long ears. When he smiled he made me think of an elf. His wife Nada was in Zagreb for a couple of days and had left notes for him in red marker: *pažni na vodu!*—pay attention to the water, *zatvori plin*—turn off the gas, *izuadi Bihinu hranu u jutro*—feed Bihina in the morning. Bihina was their cocker spaniel.

Large black and white canvases dominated the room. Shelves held books by Hemingway, Gide, Pekić, Grass, Kundera, Hölderlin, Mailer, Henry Miller, Velikić, Genet, Crnjanski, and Camus. Žarko's *Tübingen* and *Knifer* were there, as was our *Polnavljanje* (*Repetitions*). Žarko and Knifer conversed in Serbo-Croatian. Anne sat nearby and listened closely. I wandered around the room. The pencils Knifer used for his graphite works lay with sharpeners in small boxes on two long tables under a bank of north-facing windows. 9B was the standard—Faber-Castel and Cumberland Derwent Graphic. I sketched the meanders hanging on walls, leaning against walls, stacked on the tables. Acrylic on canvas. Graphite on paper. Black and white variations on a single form. We ate spaghetti with calamari that Nada Knifer had prepared and frozen. Several kinds of cheese Žarko and Anne had brought. Grapes and a melon.

Julije never talked much about art, Žarko says. A few words. A sentence or two about Malevitsch. He told me that we had to be absolutely radical with our work. After the book *Knifer* was published he praised me: you've become radical, that's how it has to be, that's it. People who visited him in Paris told me he was proud of the book, that he always kept it on his table. He told his wife Nada she should pay attention to what she said in my presence: "he writes everything down."

Žarko, you signed my copy of your *Knifer* book with a fraternal dedication:

Meinem nächsten Freund und meinem geistigen Bruder, Scott Abbott—mit Liebe, Žarko Köln, 11.12.1995

I still feel that way, Žarko says. He finishes a bite of cheese, sips at a glass of Mosel Riesling, gazes over the valley. I taste the good, dry Riesling as well, then mention that Nina Pops' work often reminds me of Knifer's.

Yes, Žarko says, those repetitive geometrical forms. I'm glad her studio is in Cologne rather than Belgrade. It's good for me to work with her.

She claims to have learned a lot from you. I love her responses to your written work, Žarko, most interestingly, for me at least, her work on your Knifer book: "Variations on the Work and Life of the Painter Julije Knifer, colored pencils and graphite on paper and manuscript pages of the book *Knifer* by Žarko Radaković." Each collage begins with one of your pages fixed to a sheet of paper. Then Nina goes to work with her pencils. She embraces one manuscript page, for instance, with two red arms. One arm thrusts into your text while the other enters a graphite rectangle rising from the top of your page, an almost sexual embrace. Another manuscript page is pierced from below by a thin, red rectangle rising out of a base composed of black and white lines and rectangles. Nina's drawings enhance the visual aspect of your handwriting and your lines of manuscript lend a literal aspect to her drawing. The intimate conversation between you sharpens my appetite. I'm tempted to write 76 variations of my own on your joint work. An artistic *ménage à trois*.

Žarko turns a few pages in his notebook and hands it to me. His writing stretches across the page in red ink, leaving three blank rectangles. Nina's colorful interlocking geometrical figures inhabit each space. Nina fills the void Knifer left, Žarko says. Knifer was like a father to me. I read my manuscripts aloud while he worked. Or we listened to Erik Satie or Steve Reich or Philip Glass or La Monte Young.

La Monte Young was born in Idaho and raised Mormon, I say. La Monte is typical of the odd names Mormons used to give their kids: La Verle, La Dean, LaVell, Le Grande. He was a descendent of Brigham Young, a man with more wives and children than he could keep track of. La Monte Young was introduced to mind-opening psychedelics by Billy Higgins and others in Los Angeles, worked as a jazz musician, and composed under the influence of John Cage and Stockhausen and Schönberg. A radical musician with Mormon roots.

Knifer and I liked his music, Žarko says. I didn't know he was Mormon. Maybe there's hope for you yet. Your photos of clouds, for instance. He gestures to the line of clouds pushing its way out of Spanish Fork Canyon like sausage from a grinder. From this deck you are the king of clouds. Your cloud stories are about process, about movement in directions that can only be presumed. We, you and I, are not conceptualists. We operate with experience, nothing but experience. Follow La Monte Young.

Peter Handke has been important to your work as well.

I discovered Handke almost simultaneously with Knifer, Žarko says. Reception theory was dead for me. I began to translate. I reached out to Handke, asked him for an interview.

I know this story. Žarko's train arrived at the Salzburg train station just before the interview was scheduled. Unshaven, in t-shirt and

Levis, he ran to the Sheraton Hotel where Handke had arranged to meet him. Hardly inside the door, he was confronted by a uniformed Sheraton employee. Could I help you, sir? she asked. I have an appointment with someone in the bar here, Žarko answered. Perhaps I could give him a message, she suggested. No, Žarko insisted, I need to see him myself. Who is this person you are supposed to meet? Peter Handke, Žarko replied. Oh, Herr Handke! Herr Handke! Please, let me take you to his table. This way sir.

I have listened to Žarko's recording of the interview several times. Handke's increasingly weary Austrian voice. Žarko's Slavic-flavored German. Meticulously planned questions. Thoughtful answers. A discussion, for the most part about writing. You are a sensitive writer, Žarko says. Sensitive is a word for condoms, Handke rejoins.

The interview concluded, Handke asked Žarko to stay with him. I'm being pursued by an angry woman, he explained. They went to a pub. Drank wine. Conversed. Here she comes, Handke said. The beautiful fury let fly a fuselage of invective. Handke and Žarko found another pub. She won't find us here, Handke said. She found them there. Exiting a third pub later in the night, Žarko said good night and went to his hotel. He heard a commotion on the street and through his window saw the fury standing in the street next to her running car, screaming at Handke, then storming away. Handke was still standing by the car when two Salzburg policemen arrived. They told him to move the car. It's not my car, he said; I don't drive. The next morning the Salzburg newspaper reported that Handke had been released from jail after spending the night there. He told a reporter that he hadn't called the policemen Nazi pigs, as they claimed. He had said they were *like* Nazi pigs.

The encounter resonates with Žarko still. He picks up the notebook with my drawings of Knifer's meanders and flips through it. Handke uses his notebooks to record his perceptions, he tells me. During that Salzburg interview thirty-some years ago, I kept trying to talk about film, but he wanted to talk about paintings. His own drawings are naïve, purposely naïve. Like his plays (he claims to know nothing about playwriting), like his novels (he despises well-trained products of MFA programs), his drawings are from the heart, deliberately untroubled by the authority of experts, of the academy, of ideology. Knifer taught me to be radical. Handke taught me to disregard imposed standards.

Time has slowed here on the deck high above Utah Valley, something to do with the distant perspectives, I think, and with glimpses into the past. Žarko and I both translated Peter Handke's *Gedicht an die Dauer* (*To Duration: A Poem*). Touched by the grace of duration, grateful to have an old friend, I bring out several photos and two drawings.

Two dark-haired young men sit at a table in Žarko's and Zorca's apartment in Tübingen. We hold identical copies of Peter Handke's novel *Die Wiederholung* (*Repetition*). Behind us on the wall hang two nearly identical works of abstract art. The shiny black table top mirrors the books and our arms. A tall house plant stands incongruously singular to the left of the photo.

Who did the works behind us on the wall? I ask Žarko. It was Era, he says. He quit painting when he left the Art Academy in Belgrade, but for our ballet performance of Swan Lake in 1976 we used a backdrop created in our apartment (a place, by the way, that attracted lots of visitors, including well known artists like Akira Kurosawa). For another work, Era attached things he took out of Belgrade trash containers to twenty wood panels; he called it "Panorama of Belgrade." After the exhibition, he overpainted the panels, à la Jackson Pollock. A few years later he used the painted panels as the basis for frottage. He liked the colorful panels but wanted to emphasize their negative reality. And thus those two rubbings.

Photos on facing pages at the end of *Ponavljanje* (*Repetitions*): I in profile, Žarko looking straight into the camera. 1994.

In 1998 I met Žarko in front of the Hotel Moskva and in the midday heat we made our way to the basement offices of Stubovi Kulture, formerly Vreme Knjige. Photos of all the authors published by Stubovi Kulture adorned the walls: Bruce Chatwin, Joseph Conrad, Anthony Burgess, Dragan Velikić, Danilo Kiš, Žarko, and myself. Žarko introduced me to the publisher, Predrag Marković, a small man with a long, full beard and intense black eyes.

Pleased to meet you, he said. You look just like your photo.

What did you think I would look like? I asked.

All this time we've thought you were a fiction made up by Žarko for narrative purposes.

There may be some truth to that, I said.

A photo from the trip we took with Peter Handke up the Drina River, an account of which appears in *A Reasonable Dictionary*, shows us at a breakfast table in a garden in Bajina Bašta. The garden belongs to Milica's grandmother, who has fed us well. Our hair is short and still dark. We wear collarless long-sleeved shirts. We are smiling at something one of us has said, Žarko so widely that a gap left by a missing tooth in his upper jaw is visible. On the table stand matching white bottles of yoghurt.

Dated 2007, another set of photos appears at the end of our *Vampires & A Reasonable Dictionary*. Our hair is greying and mine is now pulled back in a pony tail. As often in Serbo-Croatian, my name has been transliterated: Skot Abot.

In 2015 Anne took a photo of us sitting in the garden of the Hombroich Museum Island near Düsseldorf. Grey hair, Žarko's cut short, mine long. Faces lined by age, slightly bemused. Black shirts, mine with a pair of reading glasses hanging from one pocket. Legs crossed and arms crossed at the wrists. On my cheek a mark that will turn out to be basal-cell carcinoma.

We look at drawings Nina Pops made for us: about six inches square; colored pencil on white paper. Mine has a German title, "Scott und Žarko," and says "für Scott." Žarko's reads "Žarko i Scott," and says "za Žarka." Two fat parallel red lines dominate each drawing. In mine the red lines descend from top left, make a 90-degree turn to the right, and at the right edge turn back down to the bottom. In Žarko's drawing, the fat red lines are back-to-back right-angled C's. Generous gifts of friendship for two friends.

Through the years I have picked up bits and pieces of Žarko's language. A couple of years ago Anne and Žarko and I were driving through Bavaria toward Linz, Austria, to see the new opera by Phillip Glass and Peter Handke, "Spuren der Verirrten" (Traces of the Lost), and I asked Anne if she would have a conversation with me in Serbo-Croatian. Anne's Serbian, Žarko had said, was lively and serviceable.

Da, she said. Da, da, da.

Žarko glanced over to see if I was joking. He knew the extent of my Serbian.

Gospodin, I said. Anne said Gospodin and then spoke in Serbian about the gentleman.

Beograd, I said. Anne repeated the city name and then expanded on the idea of the white city.

Pivo, I said. Anne spoke about beer.

Belo vino, crno vino. Anne had a lot to say about white and red / black wine.

Slobodan, I said. Anne distinguished been the two parts of the name: free and man, and, I thought, mentioned something about

World War II, using the word rat / war.

Rat, I said, jebi ga, I said—fuck it. Anne gave an impassioned speech.

Dobar dan, I said graciously. Dobro jutro, dobra večer, laku noć. Anne greeted me back and spoke about the times of day and night.

The "conversation" continued—hvala (thank you) . . . Višegrad (a city on the Drina River) . . . most (bridge) . . . kava (coffee) . . . rečnic (dictionary) . . . razumni rečnic (reasonable dictionary) . . . pisac (writer) . . . Radaković (my friend) . . . Žarko (fiery) . . . emigracia (emigration) . . . pogled (view) . . . muštikla (cigarette holder—a word Žarko's mother taught me) . . . Srbi su dobri ljudi (another gift from Žarko's mother—Serbs are good people) . . . Sava (a river) . . . Morava (a river) . . . rijeka (river) . . . Kalamegdan (a Belgrade fortress) . . . Gavrilo Princip (the name of the assassin).

The Austrian border appeared and I asked Žarko for the Serbian word for god.

Bog.

Žarko, I ask here and now, what about God?

I have always been a *tabula rasa* when it comes to religion, he replies. My grandparents were believers and celebrated Easter festival and various saints. At the university I read a lot about religion, especially as it related to philosophy and art history. Religion was a part of culture and although I had no religious belief, I was interested in its influence. After the dissolution of Communism, as you know, my mother returned to the Serbian Orthodox religion she learned as a child. In her last years she couldn't go out alone so I took her to church. I stood next to her and helped her stand through the service. The first visit was interesting to me—I was curious—but after that it was just boring. Miloje and I followed her burial wishes and found an Orthodox priest to perform the ceremonies. I have often stood through liturgies in Serbian churches with Peter Handke and felt like I did while standing next to my mother. He makes fun of me as the unbelieving "son of Communism." I'm no atheist. I'm simply *tabula rasa*. That feels good to me. The world of the Greek gods has always impressed me, that parallel existence with them up there as images of people down here—although that idea of "up there" and "down here" irritates me.

We can see the freeway from where we sit on the deck. It runs north/south along the Wasatch Mountain Range. It has fixed speed limits, as opposed to the German Autobahn where I practiced my

Serbo-Croatian with Anne. I think of my own faith and of the moment when I realized I no longer believed in God.

Do you remember that night in Belgrade, I ask Žarko, when Handke attacked me for smiling so much?

Yes. Why do you smile so much? You are always smiling! What is wrong with you Americans? Why are you always smiling?

I didn't have an answer, Žarko, perhaps there was no answer possible. But when I think of you and Knifer and you and Handke, two remarkable photos come to mind. I think Anne took them both. The one was in Knifer's Paris apartment. You and Knifer and I and the dog are sitting on a couch, Knifer in the middle with the dog on his lap, you and I on either side, the thin white stripe of a large meander on the wall behind us. Knifer has evidently said something funny and you have a bemused look on your face as you look down at him and I have a big smile on my face as I look across at you looking down at him. I can't tell if the cocker spaniel is smiling or not.

The other photo is of you and Handke at the Austrian Embassy in Paris, where Handke has gathered some of his translators. You are sitting close on a bench, your left arm stretching behind his back. He has evidently said something that has caught you by surprise. You are about to break into a full-throated laugh and he is looking at you in anticipation, his left index finger across his chin, his eyebrows raised, his mouth pulled back in a sly grin.

I bring out another photo: Žarko and Anne standing side by side at the Cologne Train Station. My train was almost an hour late, which made the connection in Paris impossible, which made my arrival in Rennes where my son Ben was to pick me up incalculable. Žarko and Anne were concerned, concerned the way good friends who are unable to change the circumstances can be. There they stood, shoulder to shoulder. I saw them through the lenses of my camera and of Grant Wood's painting "American Gothic." Instead of a gothic prairie farmhouse window: the Cologne Train Station snuggled up to that most gothic of cathedrals; instead of a pitchfork rising between them: my luggage with extended handle; instead of a pinched face with glasses: Žarko's broad and gentle face; instead of a sideways, chinless glance: Anne looks directly at me; instead of rural American severity: urban German/Serbian concern. I was frantic. My friends stood there with me. Dear friends.

Thinking of Handke's attack on my smiling and the possibilities of retribution, I remember when Žarko bought two tiny, wood-handled Opinel folding knives in a sporting-goods store in Cologne, one to replace the knife recently confiscated from him at the Düsseldorf airport, and one he gave me as a gift, explaining that special-forces soldiers swear by this knife. The company's web site, I see later, supports that contention in general. The model I now own, however, is best suited for opening envelopes and sewing: "Les petits couteaux sont précis et efficaces au quotidien : ouvrir les enveloppes, déballer les paquets, réaliser des maquettes, sculpter le bois, pour les travaux de couture. . . ."

David Albahari's and Žarko's *Book about Music* is a work in which two authors respond separately to the same musical events. Žarko and I have twice engaged in such an exercise, first in our *Repetitions* and then in our *Vampires & A Reasonable Dictionary*, both published in English by punctum books. When the punctum editor sent me proofs for the book, she noted that much of Žarko's text is oddly punctuated and suggested that the sheer quantity of quotation marks might be off-putting to readers. I reminded her of David Albahari's assessment of Žarko as a writer:

> Even before he left for Germany and especially thereafter, Žarko Radaković was—and still is—one of the few absolutely isolated, independent, creative personalities of contemporary Serbian prose, over the years, even decades, remaining outside all divisions, definitions, tendencies and movements, without clearly visible predecessors and, certainly, without recognizable imitators. . . .
>
> And he created, simultaneously, a prose in which he dealt with his, our language like a foreign language, that is, he dealt with himself like a kind of unknown who actually makes use of the foreign language . . . in the same way, and this is my most profound belief, Beckett uses the English language and Handke the German language. In this way Žarko created a specific language, formally precise, but in fact extremely imprecise, sculptural, image based, which doesn't lend itself to the development of a story (where there is at least a trace of story present), but to the gently hypnotic state that develops out of rhythmic and unforeseen repetition. . . .

But I return to Žarko's alienation of language, which finally would be the same as if I had said "Žarko's self-alienation." For we are our language, that is, each of us is our own language, as Ludwig Wittgenstein claimed. (Or was that someone else?)

Lyn brings supper onto the deck she and I built. We lived together for fifteen years before we married in 2015. She and Žarko look across the valley and comment, through my translation, on the swiftly-moving cirrus clouds. Lyn and I have just finished a book called *The Perfect Fence*, a literary and historical investigation into the meanings of barbed wire. Writing from Lyn's historical perspective (she is an historian of the American West) and from my literary-critical perspective (fascinated by *The Virginian*, *The Grapes of Wrath*, *Wise Blood*, *The Monkey Wrench Gang*, "Brokeback Mountain," and *Ceremony*) was as difficult and as rewarding as living together. Dancing cheek to cheek—with the occasional shouting match.

Nina, Žarko tells me as we savor Lyn's tomato gazpacho with thick slices of sourdough bread, is the fourth pillar of my creative life: Era, Knifer, Handke, and Nina Pops. They are the heroes, the motifs, the themes, and the materials of my writing. You and Albahari are my partners in writing.

It was that afternoon on the Sava River, I explain to Žarko over postprandial glasses of slivovitz, that made the contours of our friendship clear to me. I wrote about it soon after the experience, leading with a thought by Soren Kierkegaard from *Either/Or*: "One ought to be a mystery, not only to others, but also to one's self." I hand him a copy and leave him alone on the deck.

Every country has its rivers. That afternoon it was the Sava, not far from where it flows into the Danube under the once-stern gaze of Belgrade's Kalemegdan fortress, far from the lesser rivers of my own American West. A houseboat was the gathering place, a rustic restaurant with no sign to announce its presence. The invitation had come in response to questions about a translation. Peter Handke had replied, in English: "On April 8th I shall be in Belgrade / Serbia. Žarko will come too, also Zlatko. And you??" On the back flap of the envelope, below F-92370 Chaville, was an Arabic word I could not decipher. A friend later told me it was "Chaville."

Packed into a little Peugeot, a big Jeep Cherokee, and a good-sized taxi, the column of friends, fellow travelers, and distant neighbors wound off the backbone of the white city. At the end of a streetcar line in New Belgrade the Jeep bumped up over the curb and ascended a steep dirt path to the top of a dike. The Peugeot eased tentatively over the curb and up onto the dike. The taxi followed a more circuitous route but found the top of the dike as well. The cars parked and the passengers disembarked.

Peter Handke tugged a dark-brown stocking cap over his grey hair. He wore a knee-length black coat, black pants that twice had been lengthened by hand, and high-top black shoes. Dark-haired Sophie Semin wore a long black coat with sleeves colorfully embroidered by her husband. Ljiljane Kapor was youthful in brown pants and a matching jacket. Her attentive assistant Marija had neon-red hair. Maja Kusturica warded off the cold with an elegant white coat and bright blue scarf. Thin-lipped poet Matija Bećković wore a brown coat and a Sherlock Holmes hat. Theater director Mladen Materić's blue jeans were baggy at the ass. Short-haired novelist and translator Žarko Radaković had no hat but was snug in a brown wool coat. A dark-haired Belgrade journalist and her younger protégé wore dresses under warm coats. And I, a university professor who wanted, someday, to call myself a writer, was comforted by a black coat against which my long grey hair looked nearly white.

The first week of April still saw the river at its spring-flood stage, making access from the shore difficult. Wooden steps led down the grassy dike to a long plank bridge that carried the party out between still leafless trees whose trunks seemed surprised to be rising out of the floodwater; at the bridge's end ten steep steps led down into the shallow water; two weathered planks reached from the last step above water to a forklift pallet; three planks continued the makeshift bridge to a gravel bank from which two steps led up onto a platform supported by four red 55-gallon drums; from that secure perch, thick planks reached onto a long floating bridge that ended at the door of a low-roofed restaurant for boaters on the Sava River—and on this day, for the eleven guests who had approached over the labyrinthine path.

We shed our coats and scarves and hats in a dining room heated by a small wood fire in a cast-iron stove. Windows looked out over the Sava on one side and to the flooded trees on the other. We took seats at a table that stretched the width of the room along two long windows.

On the previous night in the Hotel Moskva, so late in the night that the next day had already begun, so late that who knows how many bottles of Riesling including a special bottle of Morava offered by the attentive hotel manager had been emptied by the three who remained after the Serbian poet had said good-night and Sophie had gone to bed—on that night before the afternoon on the Sava Žarko entertained us with stories about a legendary pair of sly and slow-witted characters. Mujo and Haso went to a soccer game. They agreed that whenever either team scored they would drink a pint of beer. The game ended in a 0–0 tie. Let's go to a basketball game, suggested Haso. Suljo painted a picture with two naked people and took it to a gallery. It is called "Mujo in Sarajevo," he told the gallery owner. Who are the people? the owner asked. The woman is Fatima, Mujo's wife, and the man is Haso. And where is Mujo? Mujo is in Sarajevo. Peter claimed he was not a good teller of jokes but that proved to be only partially true. He said, for instance, that he was thinking about repainting Caspar David Friedrich's "Two Men Contemplating the Moon." He would paint only one man, he said, a drunk who would stand there contemplating two moons. I was halfway through a long joke before I remembered it required an English-language pun and the joke limped to its conclusion. I mentioned my brother who had died of AIDS two decades earlier and described the book of "fraternal meditations" I was writing: *Immortal for Quite Some Time*.

Peter looked at me curiously: Du bist mir ein Rätzel.

I am a puzzle to myself, I replied.

The meal on the houseboat began with a toast: slivovitz in small glasses raised to the Austrian author whom the Kapor Foundation and the Serbian president would honor the next day. Plates of tomatoes, spring onions, radishes, and kajmak cheese were the first course, served with mineral water and carafes of red and white wine. Platters of breaded Sava fish followed, big fish steaks with roasted potatoes and Serbian salad.

My mind slipped to the afternoon at Peter's house in Chaville. Had it been ten years? Fifteen? Peter sautéed mushrooms and served them with dark bread and Portuguese white wine. He gave me the first pages of the American translation of *Mein Jahr in der Niemandsbucht* and asked for an evaluation. I read a few pages aloud and then pointed out an early sentence that, in the original, ended with ". . . an der Stelle des zwischendurch mich weiterwürgenden 'Ende' das Ding Verwandlung." The translation rendered this as ". . . the 'end' that still gagged me now and then was more and more firmly replaced by this metamorphosis thing." With the throwaway silliness of "this metamorphosis thing," I told Peter, "Das Ding Verwandlung" has lost its philosophical tension. And the carefully wrought, eleven-word original phrase has been bloated to nineteen flaccid words. Your sentences have been flattened, the nuance is gone.

It had struck me then and now again that this is what I most feared about my own life, that it was commonplace, lackluster, banal, flaccid. At the turn of the century, at the beginning of the new millennium, still married, still practicing the Mormon religion I had been raised in, I woke from a nightmare in which my little car was surrounded by a never-ending cluster of identical cars that descended from the sky in ranks of ten to land in perfect synchrony and drive obediently along an endless highway just wide enough for ten little cars. I fled the marriage, left the Mormons, and sought antidotes to the unsettling dream in Handke's supple and self-questioning sentences, found succor in the author's preface to *A Journey to the Rivers* where he asserted that he had written about his journey through Serbia "exactly as I have always written my books, my literature: a slow, inquiring narration; every paragraph dealing with and narrating a problem, of representation, of form, of grammar—of aesthetic veracity." I would live with aesthetic veracity, I thought. My life would be a slow and dialectical unfolding. And I would be skeptical of my attempts at aesthetic veracity and dialectical unfolding.

That day in Chaville, Peter showed me a letter from American publisher Roger Straus to Siegfried Unseld, Handke's German publisher: "We have a problem, and his name is Peter Handke." The books weren't selling as they once had. How was it possible, I asked myself, that an editor with Straus' reputation had no idea what the translations were doing to Peter's work?

I removed the bones from my second fish steak and reflected on how challenging I found each of Peter's new books. It helped to read with a pen in hand. *Der Grosse Fall* (*The Great Fall*), for instance. I had read it slowly, fascinated by the dual metaphor of standing and falling announced by the title, attentive to the slow, inquiring progress of the metaphor. I wondered if my method was compensatory gratification for the sterile pedant I feared I had become. No, I thought. I was finding my way out of dualistic dead ends through the simultaneously critical and affirmative ideas Peter so often conjoined with "and." I had once written about this productive interplay in Peter's novel *Die Wiederholung* (*Repetition*), describing the method as "postmetaphysical metaphysics." Peter disdained abstractions of that sort.

The afternoon hours passed without seeming to pass. The courses of food and pitchers of wine were ever-changing constants as the houseboat lifted and fell with the river's insistent current. I was experiencing, I thought, a kind of standing now, a *nunc stans* in which memory was as present as the experience itself.

Peter moved to an adjoining table to speak with the Serbian journalists. Žarko joined them as translator, a role he had played dozens of times over the years while traveling with Peter in what had been Yugoslavia. I realized that the wine had gone to my head like the scent of elderberries at the Hallesches Tor in ETA Hoffmann's "The Gold Pot." Peter looked tired. The journalists asked their questions. Žarko translated them. Peter responded. Žarko translated the responses. Žarko looked tired as well.

"Or" had been my original conjunction. I spent two years in Germany as a Mormon missionary. I knew the truth and knew that other people needed it and I bore witness that if they would pray as I had God would reveal the truth to them as well. My German improved and I began to read—*Buddenbrooks, Mutter Courage, Der Steppenwolf.* Nietzsche's wild-eyed *Zarathustra* taught me that we create our truths instead of finding them. Lessing's wise *Nathan* offered a parable in which the magic ring was mercifully lost. I too would essay a life on my own terms, I thought, on my own terms and yet in the context of the American, Mormon *Volk* I had left and that was still with me even as the minutes and hours of the afternoon on the Sava were stretched and enhanced by wine and tiredness.

I admired the lively face of the man Žarko described as one of Serbia's greatest living poets and marveled at Mladen's heavy brows and enjoyed the animated interaction between Maja and Sophie as they smoked and talked and smoked. I watched red-haired Marija move around the room to take photos of the gathering.

The German writer Peter Schneider attacked my translation of *A Journey to the Rivers* for presenting Peter's work in a less controversial light than it deserved. I replied that Schneider either couldn't read or refused to read. Criticize what is there, yes; but criticize what you put there with your simplistic and inflexible mind and you become the aggressive and stupid critic I was afraid Peter took me for when he called me Dr. Scott. I am a Germanist, a good one. I am also a writer, co-author with Žarko of two books described in Belgrade as a "two-seater without steering." Couldn't a person be both a writer and a critic? Was it the double roll that made me a puzzle to Peter?

When had I begun to write my non-critical work? Why had I done that? It was Žarko's invitation, I thought. Žarko had asked me to contribute to a Belgrade journal and then to his anthology on childhood and then to the *Flugasche* issue on the painter Julije Knifer and then the collaboration on the book *Repetitions* and later on *Vampires & A Reasonable Dictionary*. It was Peter's influence as well. His books engaged me, called to me even, made me want to understand, to pay attention, to weigh possibilities—and beyond the understanding to write, to write about myself.

If I ever wrote a book about Peter Handke, I told myself as the houseboat rose and fell gently in the wake of a passing boat, I would write about the dialectical texts and certainly not about this afternoon on the Sava. I wanted to write about Žarko's books as well. I would learn Serbian, I thought, Serbo-Croatian, so I could read my friend's *Tübingen, Emigracia, Knifer, Era, Strah od Emigracije, Pogled, Kafana*, and so on. I had made that vow before. I would make it again.

The river flowed past, heaving and falling like a mother's breasts. Marija was brilliant and Handke looked tired and Sophie and Maja shared more cigarettes and Mladen gestured broadly and Matija Bećković said hello to me and in English which Mladen translated into Serbian I told the smiling poet that Žarko had said he was the best of all living Serbian poets. The poet winked and said Žarko always told the truth. I said I had known Žarko to lie on occasion. Not in this case, the poet replied.

I was exhausted after five hours on the houseboat on the Sava River. Time folded in on itself with the food and the wine and Mladen's huge head and Žarko's solicitous translations and Sophie wincing with her back pain and another pitcher of wine and overlapping conversations translated back and forth from Serbian and English and French and German and even Spanish and the poet's funny stories about another Serbian poet and soft cheese and onions and more wine. Peter asked the young journalist if she had a boyfriend and she said yes and he asked for his name and she said Vladimir and he said Vladimir? Vladimir! and fish soup came and I asked Marija with her beautiful sharp nose and bright red hair about the man in blue eating alone at a separate table and she said he had a factory that made medals like the one the President of Serbia would give to Peter the next day and, she added with a smile, he gives away a lot of medals! I said he must be a very good President then and she laughed and said oh yes he's the best there is and I suggested that perhaps the President would give Žarko and me medals too and she said it would surely happen but that it would probably require that we stay in the country just a few more days and I said we were leaving on Thursday and would that be long enough? and she thought perhaps it might

29

require the weekend as well and the fish soup was followed by thick fish steaks accompanied by potato salad and the Sava flowed as slowly and powerfully as time while swallows dipped and rose outside the window and a photo of Angela Merkel handing a scholarship notice to the son of the houseboat owner hung on one wall and Peter joined the two journalists at another table for an interview Žarko translated and I stared at a photo of a man holding a huge fish in his arms and Marija asked the houseboat owner who said it was a Sava River fish like the one that lay in steaks in front of us and, raising a glass of wine to my lips, I realized that the cold spring meant that there were no orgiastic frogs croaking the way they had alongside the barge on the Danube that night fifteen years earlier when Žarko and I sat with the filmmaker Edgar Pera and drank Jelen Pivo and pissed through a hole in the restroom floor into the Danube and I thought of the book I had read by David Albahari, the one called *Leeches*, and about the nationalist antagonisms and conspiracy theories sucking nourishment out of the postwar Yugoslav state and then we ate nicely toasted cream puffs and deliciously oily baklava and Maja told rapid stories in French while she and Sophie and Ljiljana shared stiletto-thin cigarettes from a pack that was giving out and I wondered why so many "j"s are required for the name Ljiljana and the Sava flowed unceasingly and I, politely, at least I was trying to be polite, asked Maja Kusturica what she did professionally and she asked me, in English, to repeat the question and when I did she raised her shapely eyebrows and expelled cigarette smoke through her nose and looked me in the eyes and said "I suffer." I wanted to laugh but smiled instead and she smiled back and time flowed on like the Sava River.

That night, lying alone in the dark in what had been Žarko's mother's apartment, I remembered the pleasure I had felt the previous day when I bought a copy of Žarko's translation of Peter's *Die morawische Nacht*, featured that month in the windows of Belgrade bookstores. Žarko signed it for me with a dedication:

Lieber Scott,
In Peters Morawa münden wir immer wieder ein, und immer wieder fließen wir daraus, und niemand weiß, wohin sich diese gewaltige mäandernde Wassermasse bewegt. Wir zwei, mein liebster Freund, bleiben immer dabei . . .
Dein, Žarko

Dear Scott,
We flow again and again into Peter's Morava and again and

again we flow out of it and no one knows the course of this powerful meandering water mass. We two, my dearest friend, will always be there . . .
Your, Žarko

I step back out onto the deck. The sun has set behind the mountains to the west. Žarko has finished reading and is looking out at the crepuscule. He knows the now rare word from Thelonious Monk's "Crepuscule with Nellie." It is time for me to transport us back to the island Žarko thinks I've been writing from.

Žarko sits at his south sea table, I at mine. I wonder if the slivovitz we drank in Utah is still animating his thoughts. He bends over his notebook and I ask: And you, my dear friend, what are you writing about?

Postscript:

I can't write about a friend and make it neat and tidy unless I intend to kill my friend. And this is not my intention. To be an expert on someone you know, I truly believe, is never to have known them at all.

Charles Bowden, T*he Red Caddy: Into the Unknown with Edward Abbey*

2

An Amicable Correspondence

amicable: good-natured, harmonious, cordial, agreeable, good-humored, kind, polite

No, none of those. I mean something with more bite, more room for spirited exchange. This *amicable* correspondence will be between *amici*, *prijatelji*, *Freunde*, friends.

amicable: between friends.

In 1826, officials in Weimar decided to clean out an overstuffed mausoleum that housed the remains of various notables, including those of Friedrich Schiller, who had died twenty-one years earlier. When they could not identify Schiller's bones in the chaotic crypt, a doctor named Schwabe gathered 23 skulls to examine at home. Schwabe had known Schiller, he had his death mask, but still he was unable to identify Schiller's skull with any certainty. He finally chose a skull that distinguished itself by its large size and fine, regular form. Großherzog Karl August recommended that the skull eventually be housed under glass next to Leibniz's skull in the Royal Library. In the meantime, Goethe borrowed the skull and in the night of September 25 wrote a poem about his friend, using the occasion to explore the shifting relationships between nature and spirit, between matter and mind. Wilhelm von Humboldt saw the skull in Goethe's possession and wrote to his wife that Goethe was having a burial vault built in the hopes that he and Schiller could eventually lie there together. In the

An Amicable Correspondence

end, the friends never shared a grave. DNA analysis in 2008 proved that the skull in question belonged to someone other than Friedrich Schiller.

I decide to translate Goethe's poem. The dense rhymes of *terza rima* and the rhythms of iambic pentameter are integral formal contributors to the content, but my attempts to reproduce them in English are a disaster. I opt for a more straightforward form.

> While Contemplating Schiller's Skull
>
> It was in the somber ossuary that I saw
>   Skulls aligned with ordered skulls;
>   Old times, I thought, gone grey.
> They stand fixed in rows, once mutual foes,
>   And stout bones that clashed to kill
>   Lie athwart, rest subdued.
> Dismembered shoulder blades! what they bore
>   Now lost, and fine and lively limbs,
>   the hand, the foot, scattered, disjointed.
> You lay down tired, in vain,
>   They left you no peace in the grave,
>   Drove you again into daylight.
> No one can love the desiccated shell,
>   Whatever splendid noble germ it protected.
>   Yet for me, the adept, were inscribed
> Sacred meanings not revealed to all,
>   As I, amidst that unblinking multitude
>   Sensed an image wondrous beyond imagination,
> And in the clammy hall's constriction
>   I was warmed, refreshed,
>   As if life had sprung from death.
> How mysteriously the form ravished me!
>   The divinely ordered trace, preserved!
>   A glimpse that carried me off to that sea
> Whence figures rise transmuted.
>   Mysterious vessel! Orphic oracle,

> How am I worthy to hold you in my hand?
> Lifting you fervently, ultimate treasure, from corruption
> And into the open air to freely muse,
> Turning myself, devoutly, to the sunlight.
> What more can one attain in a lifetime
> Than that God-Nature reveals herself?
> How she lets what is firm pass away to spirit,
> How she firmly preserves what the spirit engenders.
> (to be continued)

Translating the poem from German to English and from the distance of two centuries, I enjoy an expansive freedom. As opposed to my ongoing habitation in the American West where I was born and raised, my friends Žarko Radaković and Alex Caldiero live at linguistic junctures. Žarko, who emigrated from the former Yugoslavia and whose native language is Serbo-Croatian, lives in Cologne with his German wife Anne. An uncompromising novelist, he is also a devoted translator of works by Peter Handke. Alex, who emigrated to Brooklyn from Sicily at the age of nine, lives in Orem, Utah, with his Russian/Turkish/American wife Setenay. His poetry performances are legendary and his translations from Sicilian include the delightful "Bawdy Riddles and Tongue Twisters of the Sicilian Folk": Trasi tisa / E nesci modda—It goes in hard / And comes out soft—Pasta). I have been the fortunate friend of these emigrant/immigrant/translator/artists for more than three decades.

※　8 December 2017

I show Alex my new hearing aids. He points out that because his right ear is still his worst one, the fact that I can now hear through my bad left ear won't change the fact that I'll need to walk on his right side if we're walking and talking. He has some technical questions. And then he gets to the heart of the matter:

What if this destroys our friendship?

What do you mean?

What if our friendship is based on miscommunication? What if we're friends only because I've been hearing you poorly and you haven't been hearing me correctly?

While contemplating that possibility, I tell Alex about Goethe's poem written while contemplating his friend Schiller's skull.

My mother, Alex responds, had a burning desire to see her father's bones. We were in Licodea, Sicily, and she insisted that we go to the cemetery where the family crypt is. My grandfather's casket is in the ground-level room of the crypt, directly under the altar. She asked a cemetery official if she could open the casket. You can do anything you want in your family's crypt, he said. I did my best to dissuade her from opening the casket. You know how close to an emotional edge I live; imagine my mother 100 times closer to that edge. She finally acquiesced and we didn't open the casket.

When Schiller died, Goethe was 55 and Schiller 45. Goethe was 76 when he contemplated Schiller's skull. Žarko, Alex, and I are 73, 69, and 69 respectively. None of us is likely to write a poem with the other's skull on our desk.

Schiller's first letter to Goethe, dated the 13th of June, 1794, and sent from Jena to the neighboring town of Weimar, addresses Goethe as High Wellborn Sir, Highly-to-Be-Honored Privy Councilor. The letter is a request for contributions to Schiller's proposed literary journal *Die Horen* (Horae). Schiller mentions co-publishers—idealist philosopher Johann Gottlieb Fichte and linguist and eventual founder of the University of Berlin Wilhelm von Humboldt. He signs the letter Your High Wellborn, most obedient servant and most sincere admirer F. Schiller.

Goethe responds on the 24th of June and then again on the 25th of July. He offers a token of friendship and assures Schiller that he is very much looking forward to a frequent and lively exchange of ideas: "I shall with pleasure and with all my heart be one of the party."

Several letters follow and in September Goethe invites Schiller to visit him in Weimar. Schiller responds enthusiastically on September 7th, but with a caveat: that Goethe not rely on him to meet any domestic timetables. Cramps during the night disturb him so seriously, Schiller writes, that he finds it necessary to sleep the entire morning and cannot commit to anything at any given hour. "You will, then, allow me to be a complete stranger in your house . . . to isolate myself so that I can escape the embarrassment of having to depend on others. . . . Excuse these preliminaries. . . . I ask for the simple freedom of being allowed to be ill while being your guest."

And with that the friendship that proved so valuable to both men was begun. Goethe later told Schiller that Schiller had given him "a second youth and made me a poet again, which I had as good as ceased to be." Schiller, thinking perhaps of his delicate health and uncertain future, wrote that "I hope that we can walk together down as much of the road as may remain, and with all the more profit, since the last companions on a journey always have most to say to each other."

Years later, while Goethe was editing their correspondence for publication, he asked "what could be more amusing than to see our letters begin with the pompous announcement of the *Horen*. . . . And yet, if there hadn't been that impulse and will to document the times, everything in German literature would now be very different."

If the Serb hadn't invited the American to contribute to the literary journal *Knjizevna kritika*, if the Sicilian and the American hadn't begun neighborly conversations about poetry, and if the Serb and the Sicilian hadn't spoken one morning in the American's house, everything in the field of Serbian-American-Sicilian literature would now be very different.

14 August 2013

Dear Žarko,

After the afternoon on the Sava, after my experiences in your Belgrade, home again between the mountains and Utah Lake, I once again find myself between two worlds. Last night a voice in a dream warned me that I was not paying enough attention to Serbian writers. I said I was determined to rectify the situation; I would list them all for the world to see (without diacritical marks, which are especially difficult in dreams): Ivo Andric, Aleksandar Tisma, Milorad Pavic, Borislav Pekic, Danilo Kis, Zarko Radakovic, David Albahari, Dragan Velikic, Svetislav Basara, Dragan Aleksic. So far so good, I dreamt, but what of the others? Shouldn't Miljenko Jergovic and Muharem Bazdulj also be included, although they have become Bosnian and clearly aren't Serbs even though they too write in the language that once fostered "unity and brotherhood"? And if they are included, then why not the now Croatian Miroslav Kreleza, Ranko Marinkovic, Slavenka Drakulic, and Dubravka Ugresic? In my dream all these authors are citizens of a still unified Yugoslavia. And, although they now write in English, why not Charles Simic, Josip Novakovich, Tea Obreht, and Aleksandar Hemon? There, I said to the voice, I have paid attention.

But now, dear Žarko, sitting here with my morning coffee, I realize that I must have *read* them all to make that claim. Unfortunately, I'll have to read them in translation. Fortunately, translations are available.

Scott

An Amicable Correspondence

ᙌ   31 August 2013

Dear Žarko,

I found a book by the man you called Serbia's most famous poet, Matija Bećković, the jovial man in the Sherlock-Holmes hat who told me you never lie. The book, translated by Drenka Willen, includes a play called "CHE: A Permanent Tragedy" and a set of satirical essays called "Random Targets." I especially like Bećković's essay "On the Abuse of Democracy":

> How can democracy be abused? . . .
> Walking in the rain without an umbrella, being a vegetarian, a miser, being illiterate, hungry, moody, irritable? Every human has a right to be these. They can't be called an abuse of democracy.
> Standing on one foot, talking nonsense, being without talent, writing bad books, writing bad poems—all these are the prerogatives of a free man. No, they're not an abuse of democracy, either. . . .
> Is there too much smoking, too much thinking, too much writing, and too much love-making? Are these an abuse of democracy? . . .
> The abuse of democracy is the favorite topic of those who would abuse it most gladly. . . .
> There are people who still think that too much democracy inevitably leads to catastrophe—which can be delayed by injustice, by crime, by wars, and by bombs.

Žarko, I wish I could have joined you and Gospodin Bećković for coffee and conversation about democracy in a Belgrade café in 1969. I was a missionary in Cologne that year, preaching the gospel to radical German students, reading Brecht's *Mutter Courage* on the streetcar, learning the German language that has enabled conversation between you and me for almost 35 years. Our friendship is possible only in translation.

Scott

ᙌ   7 September 2013

Dear Žarko,

I've been working through my notes from the Belgrade trip and thought this account might make you smile (or flinch):

> I am exhausted after five hours on the houseboat on the Sava River, but back in the city Handke announces an evening appoint-

ment at another restaurant and off we go in taxis—Peter, Sophie, Zlatko (who has arrived on the bus from his home in Porodin), you, and I. At the restaurant we are joined by a publisher of some sort, a French lawyer, an actress who knows Zlatko, and Dragoljub Milanović and his wife. Milanović has just been released from prison after ten years. He was director of Serbian Radio and Television during the NATO "intervention" in Kosovo. NATO bombers had struck targets in Belgrade (including, by digital accident, the Chinese Embassy, and by who knows what accident, the far side of the apartment block inhabited by your mother Ljubica). Milanović had learned that the media tower might end up a target as well. He decided to keep his people working and when a missile struck the tower there were 16 dead and as many wounded.

It was a mistake, NATO said. It was necessary to stop the propaganda in support of the ethnic cleansing in Kosovo, NATO said. It was unlawful, the Geneva Convention said. It happened as part of the war, but not in the part of the war where atrocities were taking place, the Hague tribunal said. Dragoljub Milanović, however, should have cleared the building, the Serbian court said, and so he spent 10 years in prison. None of the actual killers were ever tried.

Now the former Director of Serbian Radio and Television sits quietly, even timidly, but certainly sweetly and a little sadly at a long table, his back to a flat-screen television on the wall that is broadcasting the fourth match of the Davis Cup quarterfinal between Serbia and the United States: Novak Djoković against Sam Querrey. Serb players have won two of the three matches already concluded. A third win will send the Serbs on to the semi-final round against Canada. But Djoković, ranked number one in the world, is having trouble after having won a close first set. He seems to be injured. While people speak in Serbian and French and German and English around the long table, you and Zlatko and I watch the American take the second set 7-6. Zlatko points at me and announces to the table that "HIS American has just won a set. Djoković is in trouble."

Across from me sits the actress, blond and perfect, her voice trained to PROJECT. She speaks with you and Zlatko, quick repartee punctuated by lethal machine gun bursts: da!da!da! da!da!da! I duck when the first round comes at me, but as the evening goes on I get used to the triple plosive affirmative salvos. She is acting in a National Theater production of the American play "Killer Joe." She asks us if we want to go to a party with her after the long dinner. We decline.

Djoković wins the final two sets 6–1 and 6–0.

Why, Žarko, do I record these events? Why do I find them noteworthy? That I do may be a key to who I am.

Scott

❧   10 September 2013

Dear Žarko,

More notes from the transformative stay in Belgrade. Travel shifts my perspective, provokes me with reminders of who I am, who I am not.

I sit in a cafe named Snežana or Snow White, just a block from the Laguna Publishing House where you and David Albahari are speaking with your editor about the last details for your *Book about Music*.

I order ice coffee and *voda sa gasem*. I give up my pitiful Serbian when the waiter speaks to me in perfect English. I read Momo Kapor's *Guide to the Serbian Mentality*. My coffee is in a tall glass. A straight straw and a crooked straw and a tall spoon rise up out of the coffee topped with whipped cream. I write about my coffee and wonder how the men at the next table see me. Do they see the writer at his café table writing brilliantly about his coffee?

The waiter returns. You are reading a Serbian book, he says.

Yes. In translation. Do you know Momo Kapor?

Of course I do.

Of course, I think. The bodyguard of the President of Serbia said yesterday he had read Peter Handke's *The Moravian Night* in Žarko's translation. This small country has literate bodyguards, literate waiters, and, on the streets, the world's most beautiful legs.

I always feel an erotic tug when I think of Europe—you know some of the history of this, Žarko, good friend and confidant that you are—but the long and stylish legs moving in such quantities and with such qualities along Belgrade's pedestrian streets are surely noteworthy.

Do you think of Belgrade as a woman? I ask the waiter.

Of course, the waiter says, and turns the pages of Kapor's book until he comes to a drawing of the city and the Sava River shadowed by the body of a young woman. He turns to an essay about the very café I'm sitting in: "Snežana (Snow White) . . . was the first place where croissants appeared—which was an unprecedented miracle. Croissants . . . heralded in 1950s Belgrade the beginning of the end of dreary socialist cuisine."

The waiter leaves and I revisit my morning in the Zepter Museum, a private collection of contemporary Serbian art just up the street from the cafe.

A young woman (with legs) welcomed me in the foyer and asked, in perfect English, if I would like a ticket.

Yes, I'd like to see your collection.

That will be 200 Dinar, she said, unless, of course, you are older than 63.

I asked her to repeat what she had just said.

If you are older than 63, entrance is free.

To be exact, I finally managed to say, I am not over 63 but exactly 63.

That's good enough, she said, and handed me a ticket.

I sit in the Snežana Café with my coffee and Kapor's book and confront the evidence that I'm no longer who I still think I am. Without even asking to see documentation of my age, she handed me a ticket. It's a catastrophe.

Žarko and David Albahari come from the publisher and Žarko introduces me to his co-author. The three of us sit at a corner table and drink coffee. I tell Albahari I have just finished his novel *Götz and Meyer* and that I especially like the way the narrator repeatedly questions whether he is describing Götz, "or is it really Meyer?" I speak with Albahari (who has lived in Calgary, Canada for 20 years) in English. I speak with Žarko in German. Žarko speaks with Albahari in Serbian. Albahari is quiet, reserved. His eyes dart and flash, without reservation.

I vow to read everything David Albahari has written.

Žarko, that I read is a lifelong habit. That I write is a function of my reading coupled with the inspiration I experience in your company and enhanced by your critical responses to my work.

Scott

> Schiller to Goethe: 13 January 1804

While inquiring about your health I also ask if you feel able and in the mood to pay attention to a literary concern. If so, I want to send you the long first act of my *Wilhelm Tell* which Iffland is asking me for but that I don't want to send without your thoughts.

> Goethe to Schiller: 13 January 1804

That is not a first act but an entire play and such an excellent one that my heartfelt wish is to see more soon. . . . I have three minor suggestions. . . .

> Schiller to Goethe: 24 February 1804

Here the roles for Tell, with my suggestions for the actors. . . . I have created three new women for the three remaining actors who aren't satisfied being stage hands. . . .

❧   Schiller to Goethe: early March 1804

It comforts me that you have taken on the *Tell*. When I feel at all able I will come by. Since I saw you last at the read-through I haven't been well. . . .

❧   12 September 2013

Dear Žarko and Scott,

After some time spent with your book *Repetitions*, I wanted to respond, not in any complete way, but in a series of observations which I hope you may find helpful. . . .

Given your remarkably diverse approaches to language and to seeing, your lives could only touch in an impossible friendship. And yet, there you are, together inside the dimension of those pages, talking to each other in ways that are rare and wonderful. . . .

I like this game of hide and seek: flip to 22 May 1989 (in Žarko's); flip to 22 May (in Scott's). Day after day, at random or in a series. I am enjoying this book. It involves me. I'm collaborating in a search, in a way of seeing, and in a manner of speaking. I no longer think about how you both would want me to approach this joint work of yours. I don't care anymore. I'm on a roll. Traveling with you, I want to write my own version of the day's activities. Did I say version? No. Make that my own "vision" of the scenery and occurrences, of the people. Is this another form of repetition?

You will not understand Peter Handke this way. You will not encounter him in his own past. He lives in books as much as you do. A book is a time-space machine. Handke's ghost walks into the room of your book. He sits in an easy chair and attempts to read what's left of his life in the lives of both of you. He recognizes himself as a new creature. So, is this life after death? he wonders. You both must be wondering the same thing . . . there it is . . . it all exists to end up in a book.

Alex

❧   13 September 2013

Dear Alex,

Your reading, like our reading and traveling, doesn't find what it is looking for. Your writing, like our own, simply acts. It does, it performs, it labors, it discovers (takes the covers off).

thank you, my friend.
Scott

           ❧   11 February 2014

Dear Scott,

 I had a revelation while in the hospital.

 Mortality.

 As you know, they tried to treat the diverticulitis with a long fast but finally had to take out a section of my colon. That left me, as you pointed out when you visited me (and thank you for that), with a semi-colon.

 Trouble comes in pairs. Setenay is now in the same hospital after a heart attack. Life is short, my friend.

 Alex

           ❧   26 July 2014

Dear Žarko,

 I've been "Sittin' on the Dock of the Bay." Okay, there is no dock, and there is no real bay, but Otis Redding is on my mind, "wastin' time" and "watching the tide roll away." It is late evening, darkness gathering, and like Redding the loneliness won't leave me alone. I sit at a window above the Pacific Ocean and watch a smooth wet sliver of sand reflect the last light. The waves roll in over the sand, one after the other, six or seven churning lines visible at once. Each wave has a different character, leaves a different pattern of shining sand. Powerful or less powerful, straight on or pushed by another wave from the side. Quickly following the next wave or arriving after a long pause, each wave alters the brilliant band of sand in its own way. I squint to narrow my focus, seeing only the wet sand and the dark dry sand. I want to experience the shifting form as directly as possible. Each new form is predictable on the basis of the interaction of complex forces: geology, hydrology, gravity, the almost full moon, the weather over the Philippines, the wake of the fishing boat whose light just winked on the horizon, the shivering passage of fish. This scene is art stripped to the essence: each wave a new drawing, each wave a new dance, each wave a new line of poetry. I squint again. I want to see only the dark spit and the gleaming sand. I want to see.

 Goethe's attempts to observe without mediation are lurking in my mind, Žarko. As are Schiller's speculations about art. "Two souls dwell in my breast," Goethe's Faust laments, "the one holding to the earth, the other rising above."

I greet you from the Oregon coast.
Scott

                             ❧   Goethe to Schiller: 16 April 1804

[Notes on the staging of *Macbeth*]
. . .
II.
The bell peals. May not be clinked, one hears rather a *peal*. . . .
III.
At Banquo's murder total blackout.
The fruits on the table should be painted redder. . . .
V.
Macbeth ought to arm himself, at least partially, on stage; otherwise he has too much to say with no visible context.
He should not fight in an ermine coat.

                                         ❧   1 August 2015

Dear Žarko,

I am back home in the mountains of Utah. Many thanks to you and Anne for your hospitality—as generous this summer as it was in Belgrade two years ago.

Who am I? I asked, sitting with you on the bank of the Rhine. Cologne has repeatedly stretched my sense for who I am: as a missionary, as a writer, as a lover. You once asked me to compose a one-sentence answer to that biographical question for a book of such sentences by Serbian writers.

I'm not a Serbian writer, I told you.

No one knows that better than I do, you said. But you're the co-author of two books with me and they have been published in Serbia, in Serbo-Croatian.

So I wrote this sentence:

> After Ljubica Radaković fed me chicken soup and taught me to say *Srbi su dobri ljudi*, after our Belgrade publisher realized I was not a figment of Žarko's fertile imagination, after translating Peter Handke's *A Journey to the Rivers: Justice for Serbia*, after traveling up the Drina River between the wars, after the man in Bajina Bašta said he had read our book and I said "so you're the one," after the cruise missile bought with my tax dollars shook the stove that cooked the chicken soup, after I realized that my brother's death was not final, after I left the homophobic Mormon Church that inspired some of my

best feelings and denounced the xenophobic country I still love, after my hair turned silver and the divorce was final and my children grew up and Lyn found her way into my heart, after six eventful decades I still have more questions than answers.

You and I sat on a bench on the bank of the Rhine River, about a kilometer upstream from the Cologne cathedral and train station. I commented on the power of the flowing water, on the sheer weight and speed manifest at our feet. I wondered how it was possible for this much water to flow with such volume day after day, month after month, year after year, century after century. How long has water flowed in this riverbed? I asked. Forever, you answered and I nodded my head in agreement.

Later we looked it up and found that it wasn't quite forever, although the words Miocene and Pleistocene gave geological weight to our sense for an immense span of time. The fact that the Rhine once flowed into the North Sea took our thoughts in a more temporal direction. Things change, even eternal things.

The sheer size and power and perpetuity of the Rhine overpower me, I said. First the Sava River, now the Rhein. I'm overwhelmed. I feel small. I feel brief.

I first visited Cologne in 1969 as a Mormon missionary. I had no sense of brevity then. I was twenty years old and life stretched before me with no foreseeable end. For six months I lived in Cologne, trying my best to convert the populace. We ate in the university cafeteria, a maelstrom of political activism. I still have *The Little Red Book* I bought from Maoist students. Many of the students were vocal opponents of U.S. involvement in Vietnam. Imagine us, Žarko, imagine two young, celibate American missionaries in dress shirts and ties and short hair standing in the cafeteria line with longhaired, sexually adventurous, politically radical, anti-American German students. When people confronted us about our country's war in Vietnam, we changed the subject as quickly as possible.

I had no clue what was going on in Vietnam. When I turned 18, I dutifully registered with the local draft board. And when I returned from the mission, I dutifully registered the change in status from ministerial deferment to 1A, which meant I was eligible for the draft through the coming year. Thinking back over the intervening decades to the draft lottery in which my birthday was assigned the number 198 (or was it 189?), I remember being happy that the number was relatively high. I don't remember any real anxiety. How is it possible that I wasn't anxious? Was that a function of my stoic nature or sheer stupidity? When December arrived, I received a letter ordering me to report to the Provo bus station at 6 a.m. for a ride to Salt Lake for a pre-induction physical because, the letter said, it was possible that the draft would reach my number before the end of the year. I dutifully, or perhaps passively is a better word, I passively followed the instructions and, well-schooled by my Mormon university and by my Mormon mission and by my Mormon parents, I would have reported for active duty if the quirks of war during that year hadn't ended the draft at 195 (or 186?).

Your Yugoslavia, Žarko, was not at war when you did your service. Your politicians had other things to lie about.
Scott

᎒ 23 June 2014

Dear Alex,

I've been finishing the page proofs for Žarko's and my *Vampires & A Reasonable Dictionary* (punctum books) and thought you would enjoy Žarko's response to the performance he witnessed in Salt Lake City:

> Alex Caldiero spoke with fixed eyes. His mouth supported his strong forehead. He balanced with his breath. He floated in the air. He stood on his tongue. He drew attention with his ears. He addressed the paintings on the wall with his stomach and in those 'dramatic moments' it (the wall) did not obstruct the field of vision. Alex Caldiero moved through the crowded exhibit like a centaur through bacchantes and bacchants.

In the early 1970s, as I think you know, Žarko himself was part of a group of Belgrade performance artists that included Era and Marina Abramović. He knows your business.
warmly,
Scott

᎒ 24 June 2014

scott,
please convey my surprise to Žarko on reading his most incisive piece of seeing-hearing . . . a brother under the skin.
a.

᎒ 12 July 2015

We

Dear Žarko, Dear Alex,

After fifteen years together, Lyn and I were married today. Sam Rushforth performed the ceremony on our deck overlooking the valley. Two of our neighbors signed the document as witnesses.

I send you this news accompanied by a letter Schiller wrote on this very day, July 12, in 1796 and by Goethe's response on the 13th:

>Schiller: Things are as good in our little society as one could wish. My wife has decided to nurse the baby herself, which is something I had hoped for. The christening will be Thursday. . . .
>
>Goethe: Congratulations! I hope all will be well in everything related to the new one. My best to your dear wife. I would have appeared at the christening even without invitation if these kinds of ceremonies weren't so unsettling to me. Instead, I will come on Saturday and we can enjoy a couple of joyful days.
>
>Today is an epic day for me as well; it is the eighth anniversary of my "marriage" and the seventh of the French Revolution.

Goethe and Christiane Vulpius finally married ten years later, the year after Schiller's death. I'm glad my dear friends are still alive to share the news of my own marriage.
Scott

❧   17 November 2015

Dear Žarko,

I've been reading your book *Strah Od Emigracije* out loud, alone in my room, in the middle of a winter's night surrounded by mountains of silence and heaps of snow and ice, tho where I sit the weather is warm and a sweater is enuf to keep me comfortable and awake enuf to hear and pay close attention to the words of your book until all that remains is the deep groan of a language as ancient as human breath, a great, persistent groan, a moan, a ground sound that carries the burden of all possible meanings, not limited by, but including a vast sadness of a people who know no rest nor comfort and whose eyes have seen the inevitable torment of their own identity grown monstrous yet preserving an innocence that mocks any explanation of its existence. . . . Every word raises its questions and new grammar is born and the dream of a new language begins to be realized, starting from and out of the sound-shaped meanings that are speaking together in one voice, in one mouth—mine—yours—our mothers giving birth—our fathers planting fresh crops—houses built to last for generations—for becoming human is the sole labor of our bodies justified by history and verified by a future remembered.

The gift of your book in a language I don't understand brings me again to a familiar place. It is a testimony to a fact that never ends for me: that I am and will ever remain, in one way or another, illiterate. This fact first struck me in 1967, when I was in the Rizzoli bookstore in Manhattan. As I was looking thru the poetry section, I ran into a book I could scarcely read. It was only when I mouthed the words several times that my tongue hit on their meaning and I knew suddenly that this was the language I had first drunk at my mother's breast and had spoken all my life but which until that moment I had never read, nor even dreamed that it could be read. I could not read my native language. This was a true moment of enlightenment and joy and the beginning of a quest that to this day has given me more sorrow and pain than I could have imagined.

The status quo of every reading-interpretation-translation is that we put together what makes sense out of what we know, what we already understand; no writing is completely unknown to us, even written in another language. We read and nothing makes sense, and then, out of nowhere, we recognize something, a particle, a section of a word, a phrase, a cognate, and so it occurred to me, because I couldn't do anything about the words I didn't understand or even hope to approach, that I would ferret out those words or phrases that bore any resemblance to what I already knew. There is no book that we cannot read. There is no language that we cannot understand. We create meaning for ourselves constantly.

as ever, I remain your friend and brother
Alex

🙞   1 December 2015

Dear Scott,

Thank you for translating Alex's letter for me. His words touch me and are so important. And Alex, this human being, is for me like a god-figure from the best times of antiquity. I will never forget how, that morning, in your house, Alex and I spoke so intimately, as if we had known one another for 5000 years.

Fondest greetings to you both,
Žarko

We

>< 31 May 2016

Dear Scott

For a week I have been reading what I have written about passion, preparing to continue writing. I've been fighting with the ideas in my notebook, the letters themselves inscrutable like Chinese characters. And now, finally able to continue, I have to leave. Tomorrow we'll fly to Nice and then on to Corsica. Is this a good time for new experiences?

Family life, that's how it is. "The family," after tomorrow, will be hiking.

I love you,
Žarko

>< 31 May 2016

Žarko,

Travel well, my dear friend. Hiking is good for the soul, not to mention the family. You are not the first to write about passion.

>< Goethe to Schiller: 30 November 1796

... A new work from Frau v. Staël, *de l'influence des passions,* is very interesting, a product of ongoing observation of the broad and great world in which she has lived, full of witty and audacious comments.

Scott

>< 15 June 2016

Dear Scott,

We are back in Cologne. A remarkable trip. Corsica is fascinating. When our hikes were a little precarious I thought about you and Sam and your book [*Wild Rides & Wildflowers: Philosophy and Botany with Bikes*]. Never in my life have I seen so many wildflowers. We were there at the perfect time, right after the rains. And the weather was fantastic. Not too warm, but beautiful.

So, having survived all the hikes, I was liquidated in the Cologne train station. I was robbed. My backpack was stolen while I was grabbing a bite to eat. Along with other valuables, my notebook disappeared, about 100 pages of my book about passion. Gone forever. It destroyed me. I couldn't speak for days. I am slowly beginning to contemplate the future, how to continue. A catastrophe. Reason to give up, even living.

Žarko

>< 27 June 2016

An Amicable Correspondence

Dear Žarko,

Your notebook! A true catastrophe. If I were in Cologne I would hurry to a stationer (as you did for me in Šabac) and buy you a new notebook. And then, later, a train official would hand you your old notebook in a company bag (as did that blessed bus owner with my notebook in Bajina Bašta). But I am not in Cologne. You are not in Bajina Bašta. I'm so sorry, Žarko. *Jebi ga*! Don't give up. We still have work to do.

Alex and I were talking yesterday about books of fragments—Friedrich Schlegel's *Athenäumsfragmente* and Novalis' *Blütenstaub* (Grains of Pollen), Handke's *Baumschattenwand* (TreeShadowWall) and Chrostowska's *Matches*—and we thought: why not a book of fragments from the three of us, fragments of amicable correspondence?
Scott

❦   29 June 2016

Alex performed last night for an appreciative audience. After the applause I gave him a hug and told him he was my prophet. What made me say that? I don't believe in prophets. Why didn't I just say you are my Sonosopher? "Sonosopher" would have referenced the sounds of Alex's voice, a voice so resonant that at times it stirred long strings on the grand piano behind him. He read in short bursts, his erratic emphasis shattering the meaning so I had to wait for memory to reassemble the thoughts. The poems are themselves fragments of meaning, often written before dawn and bordering on the subconscious. There is Alex in the night. There is his notebook. There is his pen. He writes. He draws. He turns to the next page. "You are too present," Alex intoned last night, "Or you don't exist." Existence is difficult and Alex is my prophet.

I send Alex these thoughts and he responds quickly by email:

"You are my prophet," the atheist said. And I wondered what god my prophecies revealed. The god of friendship, perhaps. Or the god of poetry. And what did I prophesy? Prophets must see into future events, call them out, say it true. The events I see are more of the same as have passed. . . . And if you cannot put your head around all of this, it's because life is bigger than any head, than any thought, than any single life that anyone can dream of—*tutu c'e' & nenti si cridi*—everything is (possible), but we believe such a small part of it.

I reply to Alex's email with a passage from Italo Calvino's *Invisible Cities*: "Arriving at each new city, the traveler finds again a past of his that he did not know he had: the foreignness of what you no longer

49

are or no longer possess lies in wait for you in foreign, unpossessed places. . . ."

The foreign, unpossessed places of my friends' lives.

                                     Goethe to Schiller, 22 June 1797

I have decided to turn to my *Faust* and, if not to finish it, at least to make some progress. . . . My wish at this point is that you might be so good to think through the project during a sleepless night and to offer suggestions for the whole—as a true prophet, to articulate my own dreams and to interpret them.

                                       Schiller to Goethe, 23 June 1797

Your decision to turn to Faust is, in fact, surprising to me. The challenge to share my expectations and desiderata is not easy to fulfill. . . .

The duality of human nature and the failed striving to unite the divine and the physical cannot be lost sight of. . . . In short, the demands on Faust are simultaneously philosophical and poetic and however you turn, the nature of the subject will require a philosophical treatment and imagination will have to be satisfied with being in the service of a rational idea. . . .

                                      Goethe to Schiller, 24 June 1797

Thanks for your first thoughts about the awakening Faust. We will probably not differ in how we see the work but it gives one courage to work when one sees one's own thoughts and plans reflected from outside and so your contribution is fruitful in several ways.

                                                 19 August 2016

scott,
just viewed the handke documentary you translated. what can i say? what should i say? do i dare say anything? who am i to judge? i have nothing to say. i have too much to say. but this i can say with certainty—the final 25 minutes or so were right on. the filmmaker finally out of the way, the great german writer finally out of the way, and there is peter, no longer handke, but peter, a simple rock on a shore, peter, come home to his own name, alive in a life beyond meaning and literature and family and audience and above all the politics that infest a life that would surrender to something bigger. nuf sed. you should feel profoundly proud of your contribution—the subtitles (as english) were superb.

    til later

    alex

An Amicable Correspondence

                                                       25 August 2016

Dear Alex,
I have not seen this film.
It is possible I will never see it.
But I see you.
I see you, the one who speaks and walks.
And I hear your voice, like the most intimate voice from Italian opera (Claudio Monteverdi, L'incoronazione di Poppea).
I hear.
And I see the gentle movements of substance.
With each new step further into shadow.
Extraordinary withdrawal.
Soon in silence.
In bright darkness.
I follow you . . .
    your,
    Žarko

                                                       27 August 2016

Dear Zarko and Alex,
    Corinna Belz, the filmmaker, said that Peter declined to view the film. Sophie and Amina both watched it with Corinna. I studied the film frame for frame while translating. My translations steal the eye from the images.
    I like the film. Do I like it because it is about Peter Handke? Do I like it because it is a warm conversation with a man whose work has lent structure to my life? Do I like it because he dances on seashells that line his path? Do I like it because of Sophie's earnest and careful attempt to explain the backlash against the "friend of the Serbs"? Do I like it because it invites me into the house and notebooks of a great writer? Do I like it because I can hear the writer at work, hear formulations come to his lips, hear him reject an incipient idea and try out another one? Do I like it because of the phone conversation with Frau Peters—Peter's gentle insistence that falsified photos showing his mother at a Hitler rally are an abomination? Do I like it because I enjoy hearing Peter reading from *The Hornets* and laughing at his own youthful formulation? Do I like it because of the scene with needle and thread? Because of the clips from the Princeton meeting of the Gruppe 47 and from the Vienna stage where Peter tells the questioner he is an asshole? Do I wish the scenes with my friend Žarko in Serbia had been included? Do I wish . . . ? Yes to all of these questions.

We

> warmly and gently,
> Scott

❦   17 September 2016

Dear Žarko, Dear Alex,

New books by friends of three decades.

Your novel *Kafana*, Žarko. Tavern or pub. The narrator sits at a table in the living room of his apartment, staring out the window and across the river where he sees a tall crane working in the sun—sees it as an animate running creature. Jasmina Vrbavac writes that the novel is "a valuable record of the unconscious, an entrance to the labyrinth of associations and thoughts that haunt the lucid author. . . . Along the way burglars steal the narration and become independent narrators." David Albahari writes that the novel "is an autobiographical account of the author as a storyteller who wants to leave no trace of himself in the text, a brief overview of avant-garde authors during the second half of the twentieth century, and finally, the study of the 'holy city' of European culture, the pub, where in the same breath a man can be put on a pedestal and immediately afterwards reduced to mold and mud."

Your *Who is the Dancer, What is the Dance*, Alex. The book designer has skillfully reimagined your water-soaked, sand-caked notebook. The book, the publishers write, "is based on a pocket journal that poet Alex Caldiero kept with him during a six-day river trip on the Colorado River through Cataract Canyon. Through poems and the reproduced drawings that accompany, and often house, them, Caldiero explores how we simultaneously impinge upon, and give ourselves over to, a landscape. In these poems, our urban preconceptions falter and adapt to these places we call wild."

You have always called me to the wilderness of your mind, Alex, inviting me to falter and to adapt, to grow. And you, Žarko, have taught me to value the sub-conscious associations that accompany perception. That your two books are appearing the same fall as my own *Immortal for Quite Some Time*, the book of "fraternal meditations" written over the course of twenty-five years after my brother John died of AIDS-related causes, pleases me to no end. That you both inhabit my book as characters is a *sine qua non*.

Scott

❦   10 November 2016

Dear Scott,

Thank you for the email and for your "The Afternoon on the Sava." The essay is wonderful. I will pass it on to the editor as soon as I am back in Cologne.

I'm still in Belgrade. The book fair was exhausting. My book was featured (in certain circles) and there were several media responses.

The book about Goran Radovanović's film *Enclave* was also presented. It looks good and I am quite impressed by much of it. Your reading of the film against Faulkner's *As I Lay Dying*, my essay about childhood in a united Yugoslavia in the context of Goran's Kosovo enclave, and Milo's thoughtful personal account of viewing the film work well together. I read the Serbian version, but wonder about the language of the English version. You will be a fair judge of that.

A good publisher in Zagreb, Mäander (its name from Julije Knifer's paintings), is planning to publish a new edition of my book *Knifer*. The manuscript for the new version is due in three months. I have a lot to do.

I'm meeting David Albahari today. Tomorrow I'll travel with Dragan Velikić to the big Serbian vintner in Sumandija. They award a literary prize (300 liters of their best wine) and Dragan is this year's winner. (In what condition I'll return tomorrow evening remains to be seen.)

On Friday to Bajina Bašta, to my children. Then on Monday in Zemun, old buddies, dinner in the "Venezia." And then back to Anne. That's the way it goes, my dear friend.
Thinking of you,
Žarko

             ❧ 13 November 2016

Dear Žarko,

The Sava essay was written for you, my friend. And I'm pleased your novel got the attention it surely deserves. I just received a copy of the handsome book about Goran's film and am proud to have my essay included with yours and Miloje's and the others.

The comment about your children and your dear Anne reminds me of the twists and turns in our lives. You didn't marry your daughter's mother but have remained close. My ex-wife will not communicate with me. Your ex-wife has faded from your life. You lived with Anne for years before marrying, as I did with Lyn.

Goethe's and Schiller's correspondence remained formal for the most part—they never moved from *Sie* to *Du*. Schiller could never quite bring himself to speak directly of Goethe's lover and housemate Christiane Vulpius in his letters. In one letter, for instance, he wrote that "a person in your household, I hear, is traveling to you and I wonder if that person could bring you a manuscript." A somewhat ambiguous exception appears in Schiller's letter of 16 December 1802: "I just learned that congratulations are due for a happy event at your house.... Along with my wife, I have looked forward to this and we will celebrate when we know all has gone well and there is good hope for the future. Please extend my best wishes to the little one and assure her of my attentiveness."

Three days later Goethe had sad news: "Things are not well with us. The new guest will not stay long and the mother, as calm as she otherwise is, suffers both physically and mentally. She wishes you well and feels the value of your attentiveness." The baby died on December 21. The editor of the correspondence notes that by "little one" Schiller was speaking of the little girl just born, although Goethe could hardly have extended best wishes to and assured the baby of Schiller's attentiveness. And Goethe clearly took the statement to mean his lover.

Our own ambiguities and misunderstandings, Žarko, enhanced by the fact that we communicate in what is a second language for us both, make me grateful for the friendship that generously repairs the breaches.

Scott

27 July 2017

Dear Scott,

We were in Berlin over the weekend—to see the exhibition of Handke's drawings from his notebooks at the Galerie Friese. An extraordinary experience for me. I'll write about it without delay.

Your photos of the sky are remarkable. The beginning is so simple and modest and then they grow more powerful. The titles above the photos are good additions. What I would like to see now is that the titles slowly develop into little stories—like the one you wrote for my mini-anthology of child stories. Your own stories told as you read the skies. Aren't the clouds letters? Stories with a slow movement to some possible end, one you don't know but that you sense. And someday when you're done I want to write a foreword or afterword to your book.

Our writing is like your photos. We're not conceptualists—and that includes Alex. We're not jokers. We don't perform tricks. We're not proposing something. We are substantial. Your experiences with the sky and with clouds are absolutely experiential. As is Alex's Sonosophy.

An Amicable Correspondence

warm greetings from Anne and me, to Lyn as well,
Žarko

          ❦   13 October 2017

Dear Friends,

Thinking today about our notebooks, thoughts inspired by your review, Žarko, of the 107 images cut from Handke's notebooks—cut out by Handke himself—currently on display at the Galerie Friese in Berlin. You raise questions about art produced by untrained artists. I once reviewed an exhibition of your work Alex, arguing that if you were a better artist your work would be less interesting. Handke, who recently won the Ibsen International Prize for Drama, claims he doesn't know how to write plays; if he did, his work would less compelling. But back to the drawings.

Looking at the drawings in the gallery, Žarko, you found images you had already seen elsewhere, namely in Handke's notebooks. The drawing of a shawl and cap left in a café in Paris, for instance, was originally in a notebook you held open in your hand and photographed:

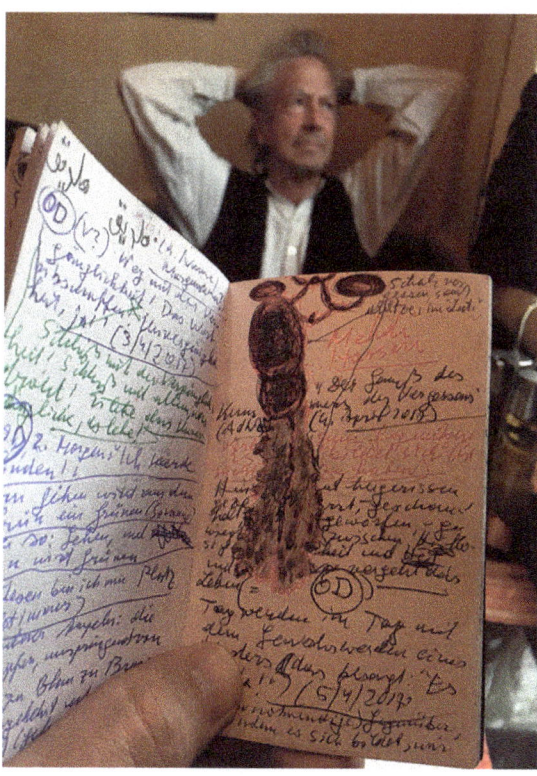

We

And my photo of you with your notebook, Žarko, complete with drawings by Nina Pops in blank spaces you left for that purpose:

Your vast collection of notebooks, Alex, are ordered chronologically and include colorful explorations I have often compared to jazz improvisation:

An Amicable Correspondence

Pages from one of my notebooks—notes while viewing Grünewald's Isenheim Altar.

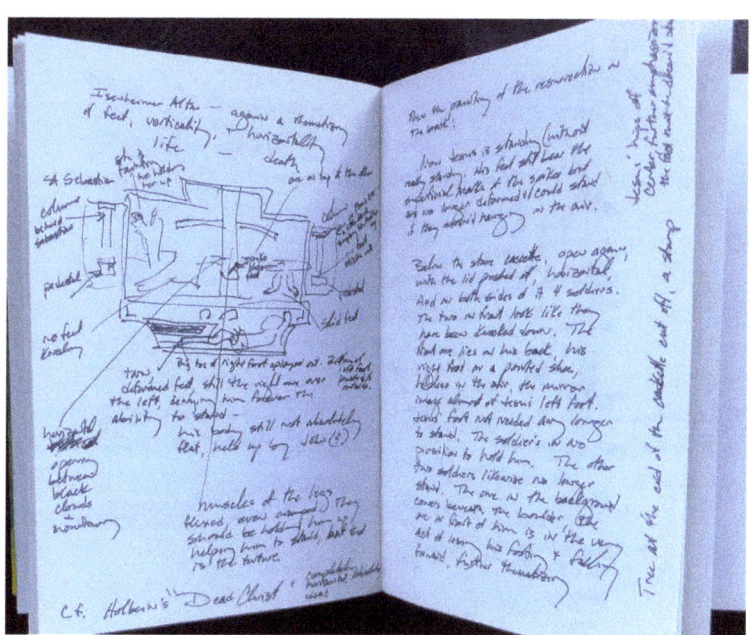

We

The way the standing metaphor structures our lives is often the lens through which I view art: here the feet of the crucified Christ are utterly destroyed.

Precious, these records of our observations and sites of our musing. I wish I could line up all of our notebooks for a photo that would represent us in a way that a picture of us standing shoulder to shoulder cannot.

Thinking of us standing shoulder to shoulder, I remember the monument to Goethe and Schiller that stands in front of the German National Theater in Weimar. The life-sized sculpture of two demigods was created by Ernst Rietschel and dedicated in 1857. The bronze, legend has it, came from Turkish cannonballs. It will be difficult to find Turkish cannonballs today; given our various motherlands, we won't be able to duplicate the German monument's contention that it was erected by "Das Vaterland"; and finally, instead of a dedication to "Dem Dichterpaar," ours will read: "Dedicated to the Three Amigos."

Scott

ॐ   14 October 2017

Scott,

As you know, Paul Klee and Wassily Kandinsky taught at the Bauhaus in Weimar between the World Wars and, like other colleagues there, found the sculptural beatification of Goethe and Schiller amusing. In 1929, the two artists stood on a beach in southwestern France and recreated the monument's pose for a photo.

Count me in for our statue only if there is a good dose of irony *à la* Klee/Kandinsky and only if it shows me every bit as tall as you and Žarko. The Weimar monument raised the shorter Goethe to Schiller's height, so there's precedent.

On a more serious note, I need to talk with you about pedagogy. Once again I am up to my neck in trouble. Last week I ordered a disrespectful student to leave the class. On his way out he turned and said "fuck you!" I replied gently: "and you your mother." The little prick reported me, and now the department chair, the dean, and the academic vice president all want answers.

Alex

ॐ   15 October 2017

Dear Alex,

You are not unique in your complicated interactions with students who flock to your classes and with the ones who flee. Let me share a couple of letters between Schiller and Goethe about pedagogy.

> Schiller to Goethe: 9 November 1803

I am hearing good things about Jena University, where some of the auditoriums are overflowing. Our Dr. Hegel has, evidently, attracted many auditors who are not dissatisfied by his lectures. . . .

> Goethe to Schiller: 27 November 1803

I have spent pleasant hours with Schelver, Hegel, and Fenow. Schelver's botanical work is so good that I hardly trust my ears and eyes. . . . In Hegel's case, this idea has occurred to me: couldn't one help him with technical advice on rhetoric? He is an excellent man; but there is so much working against his expression.

> Schiller to Goethe: 30 November 1803

Your letter reveals that you are cheerful, and I am pleased to see that you have become better acquainted with Hegel. What he lacks can hardly be given him, but the inability to express himself well is in general a national shortcoming and compensates for itself, at least for a German auditor, through the German virtues of thoroughness and of honest seriousness.

Although what follows in the letter of November 30 has nothing to do with pedagogy, I thought you would enjoy Schiller's closing remarks to Goethe about Germaine de Staël's impending visit.

Frau v. Staël is really in Frankfurt, and we can expect her here soon. If she knows German, I have no doubt that we can deal with her, but to explain our religion in French phrases and then face her French volubility is too hard a task. We wouldn't escape the way Schelling did with the Frenchman Camille Jordan, who came primed with Locke—*Je méprise Locke*, Schelling said, and his interlocutor fell silent. All the best to you.

Alex, You might emulate Schelling when the Dean comes primed with "courtesy." The moral of this exchange: be thorough and honest like a German, speak French only when you have to, and wish Goethe and Schiller were your academic administrators.

Scott

> 19 Dec 2017

scott,

i've been thinking how old fashioned i am. the very idea that art can change people, that a poem has some power to bring enlightenment—such ideas right outta the 18th, 19th centuries, romantic notions straight out of Shelly and his crew (poets are the unacknowledged legislators, etc.). i keep forgetting that the acts of art and poetry are functions of my organism, not an act of self-expression or of didactical hopes to teach, to edify, to improve society. they are, rather, the function of a breathing being who lives and changes and disappears, who exists and enters and is gone gone gone. i breathe! i sweat! i write!! birds don't sing to express themselves.

 as ever,
 alex
 yr frendly naybohood sonosopher.

               21 Dec 2017

Alex,

 Just now, after all these years, I learned that *OR*, the title of your "Book 'O Lights" (the book Richard Kostelanetz said "ranks among the most imaginative and ambitious visual-verbal books of the 1990s") means LIGHT in Hebrew. I'll be damned. I learned that fact reading a short essay about Peter Handke's novel *Repetition* by Philip Baber, the Amsterdam-based editor/publisher for whom I translated Handke's *To Duration*. He quotes a passage from *Repetition* that reminds me of our conversation the other day (and on days before): "'I resolved that at some future date I, too, would do my work so slowly, so thoughtfully, so silently, uninfluenced by anyone who happened to be present, in perfect independence, without encouragement, without praise, expecting nothing, demanding nothing, without ulterior motive of any kind.'"

 Scott

              22 December 2017

scott,

 the quote from *Repetition* perfectly states my secret wish and desire. a goal that circumvents all efforts. it is the wellspring of my doubts.

 thanks for sharing this.
 alex

              28 December 2017

Dear Scott,

 Look what your translation has inspired me to write:

An Amicable Correspondence

To Duration by Peter Handke: translation by Scott Abbott, book design by Philip Baber. Sundry observations by Alex Caldiero

Mr. Handke somewhere said that language is the first casualty of war. Language is also the first causality of writing. I have no other means of taking it in than by and thru what is given me. And what is given are words on the page: first by Mr. Handke and second by Mr. Abbott. And because I don't know German, the translation is for me in a real sense the "original."

What can a translator bring across the river Styx, that is, from that unknown country of another language? What contexts and images and words and sounds and meanings can reach the familiar shores of one's own tongue?

Ultimately, translation is a matter of trust. Do I trust Mr. Abbott as a translator? I can only say that his "critiques" of my own work make me understand it all the more. (Note: for me, critiques are a genre of translation.) There's a litmus test for translation (this from ol' Ez Pound): Don't make a bad poem out of a good poem. No matter what, this translation of *To Duration* is a fine poem. Now, if Mr. Abbott has made a good poem out of a bad poem, all the better for Mr. Handke. But my assumption is that a fine German poem has been transmuted into a fine English one.

And what of the physical book? Everything about it bespeaks the hand: its size, the proximity of the text to the edges of pages, the font…you hold the book, it fits the hand; you read the book, your hands are full of words. You look closely at text, just you, the reader, and the words. This kind of intimacy is rare in the digital-information age, where you can do as you please with the materials you encounter. Here, you are put in a certain position in which you have to pay attention to what you read and to what is given. So the design (by Mr. Philip Baber) is yet another translation of "To Duration."

What a serendipitous and wonder-filled collaboration of transmitters: writer / transmuter / designer! They work together in this book, which is both the subject and object of their labors. And so, with book in hand—read. The poem will not be ignored. Go on reading. It is important to the form that you follow where the writer takes you, for he's got something specific to say and it is vital that you bear with him on his track thru the terrain of the book. And as you walk along, the translation from Handke's German acts as Virgil to his Dante, interpreting what we see and hear at every step of the way. As I said, I don't know German. But this English text speaks my language in ways that are both plain and complex. This offers a clue to the difficulties of saying what the poet says without getting in the way, and at the same time staying in the way. The Italian pun: tradutore/traditore (translator/traitor) loses its sting. And Scott Abbott is now the guide thru Peter Handke's "divine comedy," thru Philip Baber's dark wood.

Alex

❧ 29 December 2017

Alex, you're a sweetheart.
Scott

❧ 5 February 2018

Žarko,

This won't be a good letter, just a couple of sentences to say that I am still here. Depressed since early January. Empty. Listless. I take an occasional photo of clouds, manage to see my students. Irritation is my constant state. I haven't written a word for over a month.

Schiller's request of Goethe early in their correspondence comes to mind as I send you my misery: "I ask for the simple freedom of being allowed to be ill while being your guest."

That I can write this email surprises me.
Scott

❧ 15 February 2018

Dear Scott,

You, my friend, are depressive. In my opinion you have a tendency to that. As do I. You had a full year. Lots of tension. And now you're deep in a hole. I know how it goes. Do something just for yourself. And think about your children, your lovely children.

I am experiencing a severe crisis as well. After returning from Belgrade I was sick for two weeks with debilitating fever and coughing. I recovered and it hit me again. I was in the hospital twice. Panic.

Then I travelled to Griffen, invited to the opening of an exhibition in honor of Handke. Griffen, the little village where you and I began our work together so many years ago. I didn't recognize a thing. I talked with Peter twice. The exhibition was meaningful and comprehensive. There were even several photos of me. Then dinner. Eating, drinking, conversation, silence, now and then rising to go pee, etc. Back to the hotel long after midnight.

A few days after the trip I crashed while riding my bicycle.

Too much to do. Translations. Our book. My new book. My

book with Albahari about photography. My publisher wants me to do more for my new book. What? How?

    Your commiserating friend,
Žarko

❧   18 February 2018

Dear Žarko,

    I'm thinking, as you suggested, about my lovely children. Children, Werther says early in Goethe's novel, "are closer to my heart than anything else in my life. When I look at them and see all the virtues, all the powers that we so urgently need; when I glimpse steadfastness and firmness of character in their obstinacy, and in their willfulness good humor and ease that enable them to maneuver through the perils of the world . . . I repeat over and over the golden words of the teacher of mankind: Unless you become as one of these!"

    Scott

❧   Goethe to Schiller, 21 June 1798

    It is my fervent wish that the conditions for poetic work may soon return for you; unfortunately, your location in the garden is as bad on the one side as it is good on the other, especially now that you have undertaken to build. I know this seductive diversion all too well and have lost an incredible amount time through it. Mechanical undertakings entertain us nicely while our own activity becomes zero. It is almost like smoking tobacco. They ought to deal with us like the Herzogs of Saxony did with Luther, take us off the street and lock us up in a mountain castle.

❧   1 May 2018

Dear Alex,

    Dream this morning: I look down from a low ridge and see you and me walking along a path. Talking. The sight makes me jealous.

    Over the years I have had several friendships so precious that they might invoke similar subconscious jealousy: Doug Moeller—a high school friend who became a Marine and a lawyer and a Mormon bishop and who has kept in touch over decades; Steven Epperson—a friendship that began in Princeton, developed as we wrote a personal essay under a single name, continued at Brigham Young University while we taught in the history and German departments, and then from a distance when Steven became a Unitarian Minister in Vancouver, B.C.; botanist Sam Rushforth—with whom I engaged the BYU administration in fierce battles over academic freedom and who was

We

co-author of *Wild Rides and Wildflowers: Philosophy and Botany with Bikes*, a conversation between male friends so intimate that some readers thought we were lovers; and, of course, Žarko Radaković—who, along with you Alex, has been a life-long literary and personal inspiration.

Your exquisite little book *Some Love* has turned my thoughts from friendship to love.

> Between wishful thinking and clear perception
> there is a gulf
> that resembles the mouth of all the women
> you will never kiss.

I reach for Shakespeare's sonnets, sensing a kinship. I read about a lover's lies in sonnet #138:

> When my love swears that she is made of truth
> I do believe her though I know she lies

... and then about lies in *Some Love*:

> If
> what lips say
> contradicts
> what lips do,
> which are you
> going to believe?

I turn from your

> An erection complicates the embrace

to Shakespeare's priapic line:

> ... I call
> Her 'love' for whose dear love I rise and fall
> (sonnet #151)

Whose lips will I believe, Alex? Only the lying lips of lovers. Thank god for the lying lips of lovers. And thank god for the lips of honest friends.

Scott

           ❧   Schiller to Goethe: 15 May 1795

I learned only the day before yesterday that you are not feeling well and commiserated with you. One who is unaccustomed to being sick as you are must suffer especially. That current weather conditions are not good for me is such old news that I don't even like to mention it.

Like you, I hate to exclude sections of your "Roman Elegies." I had thought that the obvious cuts [of phallic sexual references deemed potentially offensive] might be seen by readers as deliberate reticence. In any case, we can make the sacrifice required by the modesty of the journal because, when you collect these Elegies later, you can restore everything cut here.

ॐ   2 May 2018

Dear Žarko,

I've been reading Goethe's *Roman Elegies* and Alex's poems about love, thinking about my own loves. I told you once about my early relationship with an older musician, a brilliant soprano. She introduced me to the theater, to the ballet, to the symphony. With her I discovered how deftly desire and art are intertwined. I wrote about that nexus one night after a symphony performance: "The Mozart piano concerto in C and then a Prokofiev piano concerto focus my attention, heighten my perception: the graceful wrist of the concert master, the three bassoon eyes peering out of the orchestra, the tall, slender, elegant form of a woman in black standing motionless at the back of the balcony. I am fully alive." The woman in black, the impossibly thrilling woman in black—and this as I sat next to my lover. The mouths of all the women I will never kiss.

Scott

ॐ   4 May 2018

Dear Alex,

Some Love is still working in me, as is Goethe's *The Sorrows of Young Werther*, which begins with Werther thinking back on a relationship with a young woman named Leonora. I'm still thinking about my relationship with the woman I mentioned in my last email. I was only 22 years old; she had a son almost my own age. Could I help it that she developed such a passion? And yet, was I really so innocent? Didn't I respond to her beautiful poem— "The briefest whisper of a kiss"— with real kisses? Didn't I enjoy her company and even her bed? When I told her I was going to marry a fellow student she opened the door of my speeding car and almost jumped onto the freeway.

Scott

ॐ   Schiller to Goethe: 27 March 1805

Tell me how you have been recently. I have finally begun to work again in all seriousness and plan not to be easily distracted. After such a long hiatus and several unfortunate incidents, it has been difficult to get back to work and I have had to force myself. Now, however, I am underway.

The cold north-east wind will slow your recovery, as it does mine, but this time I feel worse than usual at this state of the barometer.

Would you send me the French *Rameau* for Göschen? . . .

Good luck to you, I would love a line from you.

> ⁊❧   Goethe to Schiller: 25 April 1805

Here finally the rest of the manuscript. [Goethe's translation of and notes for Diderot's *Rameau's Nephew*]: Would you take a look at it and then send it on to Leipzig? . . .

I have begun to dictate the *Theory of Colors*. . . .

Otherwise I am doing well, as long as I ride daily. When I don't, however, there is a price to pay. I hope to see you soon.

Schiller's last letter to Goethe, a long one, included the requested thoughts about Goethe's translation.

> ⁊❧   Schiller to Goethe: 25 April 1805

The notes end happily enough with Voltaire . . . but this final section leaves me in some conflict with you, especially concerning the characteristics of a good writer. . . . When you list them this way, genus and species, primary colors and color tones are all one. Lacking in your list are designations like character, energy, and fire. . . . This *heteros logos* struck me while reading and I didn't want to keep it from you.

Schiller died on May 9, 1805.

> ⁊❧   21 May 2018

Dear Alex, Dear Žarko,

That Schiller's final letter to Goethe was a response to Goethe's translation of Diderot's *Rameau's Nephew* has made me curious about the book. It wasn't published in Diderot's lifetime (after his early incarceration following publication of his *Letter on the Blind* and the pornographic novel *The Indiscrete Jewels*—jewels, in this case, being talking vaginas—he was not anxious to spend any more time in prison). Diderot left three manuscript copies, one held by his daughter, one by his friend Friedrich Melchior Grimm, and one sent with his other manuscripts to Catherine the Great. In 1800, a German bibliophile found the latter manuscript in the Hermitage Library and had a copy made. The copy made its way to Schiller, who had translated other work by Diderot, and Schiller passed it on to Goethe. In his autobiography, *Dichtung und Wahrheit / Poetry and Truth*, Goethe reminisced that he had never come across anything so "immorally moral." It was, he said, a bomb meant to blow up French literature. Goethe's translation of the novel appeared in 1805, not long after Schiller's death. The first French edition of *Rameau's Nephew* was published in Paris in 1821: a translation of Goethe's translation.

I leave you, my friends, with a line from the first paragraph of Diderot's novel: "My thoughts are my wenches."
Scott

⁓   30 May 2018

Dear Alex,
My translation of an email Žarko sent this yesterday:

I hope you are doing well. In Bonn yesterday, visiting a major exhibition of Marina Abramović's work, I thought repeatedly about Alex. The exhibition is very good, very important. Marina's works are powerful. I kept thinking about Alex's work. Performance artists! Best wishes, to dear Lyn and to dear Alex.
Žarko

⁓   31 May 2018

scott, this missive from Žarko is most meaningful to me. my heart needed it. my brain needed it. not to mention, my blood and breath needed it. it couldn't have come at a better time. i choose life, again. thank you Žarko, thank you Scott.

till later
alex

⁓   11 June 2018

Dear Žarko,
I've been working on my book "On Standing: *Homo erectus* in the Culture of *Homo sapiens*," a section on standing stones from Land's End to the Orkney Islands. Yesterday I pulled out an envelope with photos of Nam June Paik's sculpture "Celtic Memories," computer monitors and motherboards stacked in homage to Stonehenge and presenting flickering footage of those famous standing stones with a sign announcing "No Access to Stone Circle." The sculpture was in Essen's Folkwang Museum and I first saw it the company of M., the psychiatrist you and Anne so graciously hosted in Cologne several years later. She asked a friend to take the photos and sent them along.

You and Anne and I also made a memorable visit to the Folkwang

Museum to hear Austrian writer Josef Winkler talk about his work. After reading from a recent book, he spoke about Peter Handke: "He is the greatest living European writer. When I read his sentences, I start to sweat and am embarrassed by my own." We went to dinner with Winkler after the reading. He and I arrived first and he ordered a large beer. I ordered one to keep him company. Ich saufe viel Bier, he said, drained his glass in three quick pulls and ordered another one. I was happy to follow his lead. Over dinner, Anne conversed with Winkler about his time in India, about his belief that Indians were the greatest swindlers on the planet, about the brilliance of Indian homeopathic medicine. Sometime after midnight we climbed into your Volvo and set off for Duisburg, where Winkler was staying with his wife's mother. Anne drove, following directions spoken by a digital woman's precise, insistent, repetitive voice from the navigation system. The route through the heavily settled Ruhrgebiet was unfamiliar to start with, and there was road construction everywhere we turned, some of it predicted by the navigating voice, some not. I marveled that "she" could speak so certainly about conditions that were so certainly wrong. Why that was a marvel to me, I'm not sure. Links abbiegen, she commanded. Nach hundert Meter links abbiegen. Jetzt links abbiegen. The third command brought us, predictably, back to where she had first told us to turn left. Winkler kept glancing at Anne, as if the confusions were her fault. In the back seat we kept an attentive watch, trying to make helpful suggestions. Tension was high. Our suggestions were not helpful. Somehow, despite all the help, Anne brought us to the house of the mother-in-law and Winkler, contrary to his expectation, stepped onto firm ground unscathed.

 I'm ready for more adventures, my friend. See you soon?
Scott

                14 June 2018

Dear Žarko,

 I've just read Gabriel Josipovici's new novel, *The Cemetery in Barnes*. The protagonist is a translator and as I read I thought of you sitting in your study in Cologne this very afternoon translating Handke's *Nachmittag eines Schriftstellers / The Afternoon of a Writer*. On your table lies the same grey 1987 Residenz Verlag edition of the book I have. It leans against your two-volume German—Serbo-Croatian dictionary. You open Handke's book next to a page of notes you have made, prop it open under your computer screen, and begin to work. Keeping you company, I translate the book's first paragraph:

Since the time when he had lived for nearly a year with the thought that he had lost language, every sentence he wrote that was accompanied by the sense of a possible continuation had become an occasion. Every word—written rather than spoken—that led to another let him breathe and reconnected him with the world; only then did the day begin for him and nothing, at least so he thought, could befall him now until the following morning.

Josipovici's translating narrator describes a similar process:

> The first hour of work, between seven and eight-fifteen, always gave him the greatest pleasure. Even the most convoluted sentences fell effortlessly into English forms and rhythms, and he would be conscious not so much of the meaning of the words he was translating as of himself as a kind of smoothly functioning machine, rejoicing quietly in his own ability to find the optimum solution to the problems raised by the inevitable lack of synchronicity between any two languages and cultures.

Like you Žarko, like Alex, and like Josipovici's character, I know the pleasures of translation. I've been thinking, in fact, about translating Handke's *Vor der Baumschattenwand nachts: Zeichen und Anflüge von der Peripherie 2007–2015*—more than 400 pages from his notebooks, including drawings you saw in the Berlin exhibition. The book features copious quotations from his reading of Goethe, including from the Goethe–Schiller correspondence: "'without direct observation I can understand nothing' (1796)." Handke notes, with some surprise, that "even Goethe speaks once about his 'hate' (that he otherwise rejects)."

But back to Josipovici, one of my favorite writers in English (and not only because he named Handke's *To Duration* as his "book of the year" in the December 2015 *Times Literary Supplement*: "Peter Handke's long poem . . . came out in 1986 and has only just been brought out in English, as *To Duration*, in a fine translation by Scott Abbott"). Lurking under or beside or within the solitary work of Josipovici's translator is a series of troubling interactions with women—more than troubling, in fact—events that remain partially veiled by the narrator.

In contrast, Žarko, our partially veiled lives improve when, lifting a corner of the veil for friends, we lift it also for ourselves.

We

I'll leave you with Alex's poem: "Translator: Would you put me into a trans . . . later?" And with this advice: do not do battle in an ermine coat.

Your friendly correspondent, gradually passing away to spirit while firmly preserving what the spirit engenders,

(to be continued)

3

A Friendly Epilogue

Nietzsche's playful epilogue to *Human All Too Human*

>Unter Freunden
>Ein Nachspiel

Schön ist's, mit einander schweigen,
Schöner, mit einander lachen,—
Unter seidenem Himmels-Tuche
Hingelehnt zu Moos und Buche
Lieblich laut mit Freunden lachen
Und sich weisse Zähne zeigen.

Macht' ich's gut, so woll'n wir schweigen;
Macht' ich's schlimm—, so woll'n wir lachen
Und es immer schlimmer machen,
Schlimmer machen, schlimmer lachen,
Bis wir in die Grube steigen.

Freunde! Ja! So soll's geschehn?—
Amen! Und auf Wiedersehn!

>Among Friends
>An Epilogue

It is good to be silent together,
Better still to laugh together,—

We

>
> Beneath a silken heaven
> Stretched out beside mossy beech
> With dear friends to laugh aloud,
> Our white teeth flashing.
>
> If I've done well, then let's be silent,
> If I've done badly—, then let us laugh
> And do it even worse,
> Do it worse and laugh the louder,
> Until we climb into the pit.
>
> Friends! Yes! Shall we do it?—
> Amen. See you again!
>
> (tr. Scott Abbott)

We

Žarko Radaković

Translated by Alice Copple-Tošić

For Jacques Tati

We

1

Friends

(Fangen wir mit einem aktuellen Ereignis an.) Let's start with a recent event:

I spent an evening with Scott Abbott in Essen, a city in the heart of the Ruhr region. Certain events that happened when I moved to Cologne link me to it. Julije Knifer[1] and I went to the Folkwang Museum in Essen several times. We liked the layout of the artwork on display and some of it brought to mind sources of Julije's art. Did I imagine it then, or do I imagine it now, that one of the old masters who influenced Knifer's art above all was Corot (Jean-Baptiste-Camille Corot)? Regardless of how incongruous I currently find the question "What is it about Corot's paintings that attracts me?" I am happy to be in a position to mull over once again everything that happened to Julije Knifer and me long ago.

I stood before a painting by Gustave Courbet for a long time, thinking about Anne,[2] because I remembered Anne's dedication to

---

1. Julije Knifer (1924–2004) was a Croatian artist I met in Tübingen in 1986. Julije has been the central "theme" and "main character" in my books, along with Era Milivojević, Peter Handke, and Nina Pops. Keeping track of their lives is a central aspect of my own biography. Scott Abbott is my coauthor and friend. The desire to write about our friendship dates way back. Writing about our friendship starts right here.

2. Annerose Kister is my wife. In *The Book about Music*, I had "imagined" that we met at a Naked City concert and had been together nonstop since then . . . This reminds me of Julije and Nada Knifer . . . And my parents as well, actually—the poet Raša Livada looking at them together, arms around each other, on a bench on the quay in our city of Zemun.

that unusual painter's art. And because I was already skilled at dealing with "incongruities," I was able to avoid all "superfluous" questions.

Although the paintings in the exhibition rooms at the Folkwang Museum were meticulously displayed to suit every visitor, Scott and I wandered, so to speak, from room to room. We appeared, to each other, lost. As though, against our will, we found ourselves in an unknown, vast, quite impenetrable, dense forest. If we stopped in front of a painting, we looked, at least to each other, as though we were tucked into the farthest corner of the enormous building, or had accidentally strayed into a field choked with grass and weeds that not even the tiniest bird could traverse. Gazing fixedly at a painting by Carl Gustave Carus, the 19th century master from Leipzig, I felt cut off from the world, a hopelessness that could only overcome someone who had wandered into an unknown region, and I thought: couldn't the setting in which Scott and I find ourselves be ideal for telling stores? "How do you feel?" I asked Scott, while at the same time one eye looked "discreetly" at a painting by Caspar David Friedrich. Suddenly, in the tangle of shapes and colors on "that" canvas by the German painter, it seemed that I could recognize parts of a story I had yet to begin. It seemed that "here," "right here," I could start writing a story about anything whatsoever. One such story could have been about my friend wandering through a landscape undefined by either space or time that was "determined," perhaps, solely by paintings. He crossed from one painting to another, each time surprised when a new one appeared. By turns it was the street of an unfamiliar city, the wilderness of an unspecified region, a row of windowless rooms connected by wide-open doors through which my friend passed, first fleeing from one room to another, and then entering one from another, quietly and guardedly. As the narrator of that story, I felt sovereign, of course. I was sitting in a soft armchair, with a notebook on my knees, and, with my best penmanship, I wrote lines of text like notes of music that I was simultaneously composing and interpreting. One of those triumphant moments of art when we were all synchronized: the narrator, protagonist and reader of the story that unfolded so naturally, so logically, so eloquently. And that could have continued for a long time. We could have felt that we shared a long and happy life.

One evening "we," the Protagonist of this story (Scott Abbott) and its Narrator (my humble self), happened "by accident" to be in an unknown town. We had travelled "there" seeking any sort of material proof that the Third: our common Protagonist (Peter Handke), had stayed "there."

As always when arriving at an unfamiliar place, the first thing I did was look for a place to spend the night. The hotel was located on the edge of the central "district." Yes, it was a big town, divided into rather large sections that spread in irregular geometric shapes. The map in the brochure provided at the hotel reception indicated that walking through town was possible only for short distances.

"On the ground," i.e., the first time we went into the town, the streets in the center turned out to be a dense tangle, a network of tiny streets that made you feel more "trapped" than free. Walking seemed like aimless wandering. Moving that way, even your body felt like some sort of burden you were just carrying somewhere, a superfluous weight that was impossible to get rid of.

Not even the weather was favorable to our "search." A strong wind scattered every trace. If we caught a whiff of our Protagonist's scent, it was immediately overwhelmed by a wave of fumes from one of the restaurant kitchens on the narrow streets. Everything appeared to be in order, because, for example, two people were sitting quite docile and harmless in front of the entrance to a restaurant and suddenly, after the woman smiled charmingly at a passerby, the man opened his mouth, not to say anything, but to yawn. Then the tiny street surged with odors so foul that we, the Seekers, not only lost our orientation, but also forgot why we had come "this way" at all. Abruptly our "scent tracking" turned into furious darting glances all around, but what we observed was of no help whatsoever. Neither of the Seekers, either individually or together, was able to relate his observations to anything. If he looked at something, he did it inadvertently. I "inadvertently" caught sight of a woman stopping in the middle of the street to light a cigarette, but I perceived the man who came up to her with a lighter as an old geezer who had picked up a rock from the ground and was ready to throw it at us (the Seekers). I even shouted, "Watch out!" or rather, I spoke because I was delighted by a dog tugging on a leash; at that moment, without knowing "why," I felt like a dog lover; I, who otherwise have always "preferred" cats. Scott, in an extreme state of sensuous derangement, turned "out of the blue" toward a shop window where he not only saw none of the goods on display—aids for the handicapped—but was obstinately trying to recognize, in the reflection of the passersby on the window, "someone" from the poetry of Austrian poet Rainer Maria Rilke. At such moments, only Anne remained unruffled. She said, "Let's sit somewhere and have a cup of coffee."

As often happens when the senses are muddled, feelings did not "suit" what was observed. Scott, for example, as he gazed at me, was beaming with joy, perceiving me as the protagonist of a segment of his autobiography in which he was the rescuer of both himself (from some great misfortune) and the audience (for example, in a movie theater) that was applauding both the rescuer (for example, the hero of the movie) and himself (Scott, the moviemaker). I, however, looking around, experienced the "manifestation of the Vampire" (described in Scott's and my book of the same name); I also saw myself quite deformed; I saw beings that could no longer be human; instead of two "handsome men," I saw toothy monsters; instead of two nice looking guys, I saw horny freaks; instead of rosy-cheeked young men, I saw that well-known vampire apparition: icy, pale-faced butchers; and "suiting" such observations, I felt "awful." . . . In such situations, only Anne remained unruffled. After we "finally" entered a restaurant and sat down, she said, "I'd like a decaf, how about you?"

It was no different inside the restaurant. As though we had not entered some place. As though we had just turned off our path. It was as though we had entered a cave, or a tunnel, or some structure by the wayside, a room that to our ("deranged") minds resembled the inside of a bunker, or guardhouse, or even a cattle pen.

There were not many people in that large room, however. We seemed to be the only guests in the "eatery." And everyone was (we were) sitting. Even the musicians were sitting on chairs on something that resembled a podium, a makeshift elevation made out of boards, now worn, warped, rickety, and squeaky, of course. And the "few" other "restaurant guests," if there were any, sat without moving, like pieces of stage scenery, ancient furniture, abandoned chairs, peeling benches, wobbly tables with uneven legs, a threadbare rug with curling edges, a coat rack with every other hook missing or loose, cupboards along the walls from which old porcelain cups, plates, bowls, and vases shot angry glances at us like the heads of dusty stuffed birds, while the real stuffed birds, attached to the walls, looked like the mummified heads of us, the guests, as we read newspapers, books, magazines, or old yellowed posters on the walls. And we, the guests, seated at separate tables (as usual in that restaurant), each one alone, seemed not only to be separated from each other, but also to be "someone else," in some other time, or in some other story, even that one by Peter Handke known as *The Moravian Night* (why not?). One of them, a man in an ordinary, smoothly pressed striped shirt, turned toward the musicians' podium, listened to them carefully, and they, the four of them, if my memory serves me correctly, were playing Brahms or Mozart—one of them looked like the Viennese writer Heimito von Doderer who, if he ever walked into that restaurant, acted like he was sitting comfortably on the stone staircase of the Strudlhof one warm summer evening. One guest, an older woman with short hair brushed smooth, with a little hair clip on the side, wearing a thin woolen top, an ecstatic expression on her face that perfectly suited the harmony and rhythm of the music being played, acted like a lady accompanying one of the "local counts" to a reception . . . long ago. Scott, sitting at a table in front of a wall right across from the musicians' podium, although he was wearing a light cotton shirt with rolled up sleeves and unbuttoned top buttons, leaning casually against the back of the bench along the wall, seemed, as he read the menu, to be Thomas Bernhard "in person" reading his daily newspaper at *Bräunerhof,* his favorite restaurant, now elegantly dressed in a gray Lister suit and beige poplin shirt. I, however, in such moments of "relaxing at a restaurant" (was it really the *Bräunerhof*?), in a wrinkled and worn-out, of course, and faded t-shirt, sweat marks under my arms, but nevertheless smoothly shaved, wearing reading glasses even though I was not reading any manuscript, a bit stiff, concentrated, but not frozen as I read the expression on Scott's face at the table next to me, acted, or that is how I felt, like Peter Handke "in person," although he, I thought at the time, had never sat in that restaurant (*Bräunerhof*?), albeit, I imagined, he had gone inside once but rushed out immediately with a look of disgust on his face. Only Anne, smiling and "natural," sitting facing the entrance, acted and indeed really was "normal." Anne was "there" as "herself in person"; although, had she wanted, she could have been perceived as Queen Sisi, or Maria Theresa, or even Marie-Antoinette. I listened to the music by Brahms or Mozart echoing from the podium, imagining Charlie Chaplin as a waiter in a Viennese restaurant, while Scott heard it as blaring noise, swearing nonstop because it distracted him as he wrote down the details he noted in the restaurant, and Anne heard it as being by Handel or Charpentier. "Shall we have something to drink," she said after a long silence.

Scott (I already said) was studying the menu. He was silent. He acted like someone who was disturbed by silence as well. When he finally spoke, he was inaudible. I perceived his speaking visually, the opening, closing, and twisting of his mouth. I read his lips as curses directed at the silence. As time passed he withdrew more and more into himself. His face became colder, even though his cheeks and ears were increasingly red. At one point his earlobes turned blue. The redness in the upper part of the ear went white. The next moment I perceived Scott's ears as being a tricolor flag, first like the French, then like the Russian, then like the Republic of Serbia. Then the hole in his ear, the opening leading toward the suddenly visible eardrum, looked like a five-pointed star. Now it was the flag of the Socialist Federal Republic of Yugoslavia. I was naturally overcome by nostalgia. I got excited. I started to sneeze. My chest hurt inside. I coughed. I took deep and fitful breaths. I hiccupped.

That is when the waiter appeared among our tables. He looked like Heimito von Doderer himself. (Or like Thomas Bernhard). Or like Charlie Chaplin. A wide variety of quiet, but pointed, expressions crossed the waiter's face: glaring, gazing tearfully at each individual guest, dispensing smiles, showing consideration, loyalty, and respect; and he spoke, quite audibly, with a bit of an opera diva's voice, but also with the sound of the cello from the podium, and with the rustle of the wind that came from the street: "May I take your order?"

Outside, it was windy.

I walked guardedly, moving zigzag. I walked on my tiptoes. Thus softly, inaudibly.

At the corner of two streets—one was wider, full of pedestrians, congested with parked cars along the edge of the pavement, the other, the one I was on, was empty, and the only passerby on it was me—I encountered something that I still cannot explain today.

To be specific, whether it was due to the sudden change in light—since the narrow street I was on was completely in the shade and considerably darker—I was somehow knocked out of the time and space in force "then" and "in the past." The corner between the two streets was like a gate at the entrance to a very different world. Although I still had both feet "on my" street, it seemed that I could go up to the corner and peer around it to a section of the "main street" in the town of Bajina Bašta in Serbia in the Balkans. I was sitting "there" on the terrace of Drama café, drinking "Turkish coffee," with a notebook on the knees of my crossed legs, writing "this story." Of course, in the story I kept to what I was experiencing in my immediate surroundings. I surrendered to the sensory perception of everything suggested by shape, color, fragrance, taste, sound, or any other quality. I reacted to my story with my feelings. I mused, inspired by it and by them. I weighed everything in my mind, including all my reactions. And like the greatest craftsman, I created the episodes of this story.

The story "there," in Bajina Bašta, was about a mother and her young son walking slowly down the median strip, off-limits to vehicles. The boy was wearing mismatched clothes, clothes not meant for him; the color of the pants, little coat, and hat were so different that as I looked they made me think of some paintings by abstract artists; and looking at the boy's shoes—bright red tennis shoes that were too big for his small feet—made me think of the bricks strewn around the yard of a house I had passed a few minutes before.

"There," in the scene before me, it was noon. Not even a breath of wind. In spite of the clouds, the light was bright. Infrequent passersby were followed by milky-pale shadows. I thought of some indistinct dreams of recent nights. I remembered myself, who did not have to be me.

In such circumstances, objects and living beings appeared unusually plastic. In particular, the treetops were clearly visible. Every leaf, every branch, bumps on the bark of the trees, sounded persuasively like instruments being played with great expression. I heard a symphony of the moment of my secret existence in Bajina Bašta. The harmonization of tones was so strong that I felt part of a perfectly tuned orchestra. The infrequent voices of the even less frequent passersby, most often shouts of greeting, swearing or laughter, were heard like the arias of singers who entered "the stage" pointedly, theatrically. The café's terrace where I was sitting was also the scenery of a production in which politics, economics, sports, and, of course, neighborhood relations were discussed in recitative. When there was a sudden downpour, it smelled of newly blossoming lindens. A rooster's ringing crow was heard as the bell of a cyclist doing "figure eights" along the empty pavement. Under my palate I felt the rather muddy taste of ripe melons. The tip of my nose started to itch. Although silence never reigned at any time, the master of the "situation" in which we were all on a street in the center of Bajina Bašta was some immensely vast region where, in spite of the civilized state, nature called the shots. Those present included, in addition to my humble self, a waitress (with a turned-up nose, upper lip thicker than her lower lip, long thin legs, huge bent thumbs), a taxi driver (leaning on an open door), a hairdresser (with curlers in her hair, a cigarette dangling from her mouth, staring at a man in front of the window of the hardware store "next door"), and the man (standing in front of the hardware store window, staring at the hairdresser at the entrance to the beauty shop next door).

In the early afternoon, rain started and stopped "for the umpteenth time." Large drops drummed like percussion instruments on the leaves atop the linden in front of the entrance to the beauty salon. Water spattered off the leaves of the chestnut tree in front of the entrance to the hardware store, spreading aloft reflections of primal forest mist. Water flowed in a stream through the tube of a rolled up, unopened young leaf as though down a drainpipe right onto a dog, now standing still on the spot it returned to at the end of every cloudburst to seek shelter under the eaves over the café terrace. From the ends of the ribs of the umbrella that the mother opened as soon as it started raining, drawing her child close to her, drops poured as from a spout. As they did from the large and pointed nose of the cyclist who was still zigzagging on the pavement, leaving tire marks behind him as though he were writing letters and numbers: *8, v, zero, 06, a,* etc. It goes without saying that in such a downpour the hairdresser's soggy cigarette was immediately extinguished. The face of the man in front of the hardware store window was gleaming, sprinkled with raindrops like dew on a shiny apple. Sitting under the eaves on the café terrace, the tops of my shoes got wet, because, after the sudden downpour, I had not pulled them under my chair in time, "leaving" them "outside" right where the rain was spouting from the end of the awning above. The taxi driver, before the storm began, looking not inadvertently at the sky and the thick dark clouds, jumped into his vehicle "at once," "not waiting an instant," knowing full well what would come next, and, without closing the door, turned on the windshield wipers as soon as the first drops, instantly large and heavy, fell.

"Come here and stand under the umbrella with me!" said the mother to her child in a slightly shrill voice, in any case agitated.

"God, give us more rain!" shouted the cyclist in a deep, resounding voice, in any case solemn and delighted.

"What a downpour!" said the man in front of the hardware store through clenched teeth in the voice of a hoarse ogre, in any case "unpleasant."

"Let me pet it a little, Mama!" shouted the child, escaping from his mother's arms and rushing toward the dog lying on the sidewalk, his voice tearful, in any case keyed up and excitable.

"Rain, sun, rain, sun," whispered the hairdresser, turning slowly on a dime, ready to walk into her beauty shop, with the voice of someone who wanted so say something else, in any case something enigmatic, without taking her eyes off the man in front of the hardware store.

"So, those are events on a rainy afternoon in Bajina Bašta!" I thought, but did not say, and if I had spoken it would have been with the voice of an omnipotent narrator, in any case getting on my own nerves. The whole time I kept my eyes on the taxi driver who was still sitting in his car with the door open, opening and closing his mouth, making various faces, obviously singing along with the music he was listening to on the radio. Were the windshield wipers moving to the beat of the music?

And suddenly, as though scalded by hot water, the dog jumped up, as though rousing from a deep sleep. And he started barking, in a hoarse voice, in any case unpleasant. And he squealed sadly, at any rate poignantly. Woebegone and frightened, he ran across the street and sneaked under the eaves where I was sitting, and all at once was self-confident, and sat at my feet as though making himself at home; in any case, I felt his faithfulness.

In the early afternoon (somewhat later), a car (in spite of "that" street being off-limits) stopped in front of Drama café's terrace (right in front of me) and out of it (in front of me, facing me) stepped: Woman.

She was wearing a yellowish-green suit. White net gloves covered her hands. Her bushy, long blond hair was swept up into a large, "preponderant" knot. Her bare legs were waxed and she wore "elegant" leather shoes the color of pink champagne, with high heels. A high forehead with smooth skin rose above bushy eyebrows, darker ends added with a pencil over large almond-shaped blue eyes, feline, eyelids opening and closing at an elusive rhythm, which certainly could have seemed like sending and receiving signals. Her attractive nose, neither large nor small, spoke for itself. And it was aligned with her perfectly shaped lips, painted with pink lipstick, just like the aforementioned shoes. Her chin descended softly toward the motionless, barely noticeable rolls of the double chin that flowed gently to her throat and onward to a possible neck. This fleshy wave swelled with the upper part of her breasts and plumped up, sagged down, rolled and broke, vanishing along with the heavy and light, soft and hard, quiet and roaring mass of her breasts into the ends of her décolleté, sinking into the depths of her fragile, slender, sturdy, plastic body with all its lumps, bumps, bulges, cuts, wrinkles, knots, smooth petals, inclines, plateaus, spheres, holes, and furrows. Woman got out of the taxi with slow movements of her torso, legs, and hands. She slipped out of the back seat of the car and stepped onto the pavement.

Dog at my feet suddenly started barking, no longer hoarsely, but with a crystal-clear bark.

The bicycle brakes squeaked, but not squeakily, rather like the authoritative, always composed, so reliable, soothing sound of the cello.

"Mama!" shouted Child, but not tearfully, and not like someone in despair from an unhappy childhood, or imprisoned in a cage of inadequate parental care, or the victim of excessive motherly love, rather sweetly, good-naturedly, well-manneredly, and unafraid of the unknown.

Man in front of the hardware store, already crossing the threshold to enter, suddenly stopped, turned toward the street with a jerk of his head, and gazed into the distance, and his eyes no longer held nails, screws, pliers, hammers, chains, and drills, but longing, warmth, and the need for love.

Hairdresser, now inside her beauty salon, quickly went out again, a new cigarette already lit, and looked down the street with clear, rather severe, but above all curious eyes.

I, however, watched everything happening right then on the street, and not only saw every detail perfectly, but also reacted to it at once, excitedly, intimately, and even physically, not just spurred on by the nearness of Dog that had now come quite close to my feet (shins).

Taxi Driver, the car door open by his seat and window down, the distinct sound of a hit song playing on the radio, smiled so heartily and warmly that even the broken front tooth under his injured upper lip flashed as though transmitting the friendliest greeting, and the bruise under the bloody white of his eye gave the face of that otherwise "robust" male a large dose of femininity.

Woman, of course, turned around coquettishly, pursed her lips, moved the tip of her nose almost imperceptibly from some primordially delicate equilibrium, smiled with a row of pretty front teeth, and then walked with the firmest, at the same time softest, stride, swinging every part of her body, individually but also simultaneously, bending at the waist, swaying her hips, picking up her feet, moving her sides, rubbing her thighs together, undulating her "rump," switching her derriere, kicking her heels, shaking her breasts, mixing into the picture our visions of her details with those in the landscape, panorama, from a bird's-eye and frog's-eye view. Her lips, of course, were half-open. A bit apart. Just enough to let hot breath out of the small opening.

When the wind suddenly picked up, the top branches of the linden, chestnut, Serbian spruce, and beech trees were forcefully bowed.

Dark clouds loomed over Bajina Bašta.

Rain began to pour.

Taxi Driver did not close the door to his car, but he did roll up the window. This, however, had no effect on the audibility of the music coming from the radio. It goes without saying that he was singing along with the music; this was not heard outside the car, but the driver could be seen opening and closing his mouth. He turned on the windshield wipers. Did they wipe the raindrops off the windshield to the beat of the music? The driver nodded his head to the beat of the music. And looked at the woman who had just arrived and was walking away from the car.

Hairdresser, standing just half-a-step in front of the beauty shop's threshold, was "caught" by the sudden downpour: after one puff, her just-lit cigarette was extinguished by a sheet of advancing rain. It was so wet that there was no question of relighting it with the flame of the just-lit match. There was nothing Hairdresser could do but stand there a few more moments and look at the newly arrived Woman. After these first few moments of being dumbstruck, Hairdresser tossed her wet cigarette butt on the sidewalk in front of her door.

The downpour seemed to be strongest in front of the hardware store. Raindrops appeared to have drawn an almost opaque curtain over the entrance to the store. The man in the doorframe was hardly visible. He was barely discernible. There was a feeling that he was staring out. There was a feeling that he was gaping at the newly arrived Woman. But there was also a feeling that he was watching Hairdresser's movements out of the corner of his eye. There was a feeling that his eyes were once again filled with nails, hammers and drills. It was now raining cats and dogs.

On the sidewalk, under the linden tree: an open umbrella held by Mother with her Child pressed against her, bodies shivering from the cold as though there was no protection. Rain, augmented by water pouring off the totally drenched leaves of the tree, seeped through the already damaged fabric of the umbrella. Mother's and Child's clothes were soaked through in an instant. The wind, blowing stronger and stronger from below, threatening to turn the umbrella inside out, blew through bodies trembling from the cold. They seemed to be sinking in the waves of a flood. Was there a cry of "Help me"? Did the New Arrival turn toward the afflicted?

Meanwhile, the cyclist was thoroughly enjoying his ride in the pelting rain. His tires ripped through deeper and deeper water on the pavement. He swept through all the larger puddles on the road. He sprayed more and more water. He made waves that went high over the curb, surfing on them, going down and then up again, high, high above the tops of the linden, Serbian spruce, chestnut, and beech trees. Of course he was whooping with pleasure, whistling impishly, darting glances around him, as he stared, all important and full of himself, at New Arrival.

Throughout the downpour, Dog and I, protected under the eaves of the café terrace, were sitting contentedly. Undisturbed by rain, warmed by the sun that was already breaking through the clouds, we were filled with the most pleasant feelings. And we laughed uproariously. We told each other jokes. We clapped our hands or paws on each other's shoulders. We were having a great time.

Newly Arrived sat next to us, of course. She made herself comfortable at our table. She took off her shoes, put her feet on an empty chair, unbuttoned her soaking wet suit jacket, and even unbuttoned the button on the side of her skirt. She was drying her wet clothes. She was steaming. She stretched with pleasure. She enjoyed being with us. Because Dog, who always rose to the occasion, smiled politely and asked quite charmingly: "Would you like something to drink?" I, quite the "gentleman" that day, helped the lady unzip the zipper under the already unbuttoned button on the side of her skirt. And I called the waiter in a warm, slightly "dark" and ideally hoarse voice. I ran my fingers through my hair. I squared my shoulders. I clapped my hands. I said to the waiter: "A bottle of mineral water, if you please!" I thought: "I understand perfectly well why Peter Handke always 'takes a break' when he is headed somewhere specific. When he is practically within reach of the place, he sits somewhere for a long time. He postpones his arrival. Prolongs the trip. Drags his feet getting there. He shifts his attention from the goal to just Traveling and the Road."

Dog, a somber expression on his muzzle, gave a crystal-clear bark.

Woman, now completely at ease, put her hand on the dog's head, scratched between his ears, and for a moment closed her eyes.

I continued with my musing: "Even Julije Knifer, after lengthy, repeated priming of a canvas, would suddenly stop working, put down his brush, sit in an armchair, reach for a bottle of beer, take a small sip and look into the distance. Few people knew that at such a time Julije usually sat with his legs crossed. Few art historians today know that at such moments Julije most often held his hand behind his head."

Dog yawned. His tongue fell out of his open muzzle. He gave a muffled yelp. He whined. Did he address me then? "You never write about historical events. You never tell stories about things that really happened. Even if something you write about never took place, you don't write about it like something that has just happened, or that will happen sooner or later. No. What you write about always leaves the impression of being something that might possibly have happened, be happening, or will happen. So, what you write about always seems invented. Something unreal. But not false. By no means untrue."

In the meantime, Woman had stripped down to her underwear. One foot was raised to the top of the neighboring table. Both hands were down between her thighs. Her breasts, no longer constrained by the tight bra, hung freely above her lap where the silky fabric of her undies blazed under the strong sunrays. Even though it seemed she was napping, she spoke very clearly, very audibly, with a slightly hoarse voice, and so, coquettishly, addressed Dog: "Do you have a cigarette?"

Woman's utterance immediately agitated Dog. Roused from his lethargy, additionally excited by the smooth skin on Woman's calf where his muzzle was nestled, Dog yawned loudly, opened his jaw wide, and licked the waxed skin on Woman's shin with his soft, wet tongue. The next moment he barked. Stridently. Several times, at regular intervals.

A flock of wild ducks flew over the top of the chestnut tree under which we were sitting.

On the roof of the house with the café terrace in front of it, a cat moved gingerly.

I stab a piece of cheese with the tip of a toothpick. I have already dressed the salad on the plate between the bottle of wine and mineral water. I breathe deeply. I laugh. I read the newspaper.

The sun over Bajina Bašta is now strong and vibrant. The few clouds left in the sky after the rain have been pierced by penetrating sunrays and in a few moments will be dispelled and "scattered."

Shade from the dense crown of the chestnut tree over Drama's terrace thins, shadows tremble under the pressure of ever stronger light. The scene heats up. Chestnut leaves start talking under the embers of the hot sunrays. It is noon. Scott Abbott, Dog and I. The only guests in the café. I am wearing bathing trunks and a necklace of dried and faded shells. Dog, naked, has sunglasses. Scott has on earphones, pirate earrings in his earlobes, a shaven head, and tattoos on his upper arms.

In front of Drama's terrace, the usual sight: Mother and Child on their afternoon stroll. On the pavement Cyclist, riding "figure eights" around pinecones on the asphalt. In front of the entrance to the beauty salon, Hairdresser is gazing at Cyclist, hands on her hips, standing astride, smoking a cigarette. Middle-aged Man, wearing a straw hat, walks toward the entrance to the hardware store on the corner of the street. He stops. He looks at Hairdresser for several moments. Neither his eyes nor his depraved mien can be seen through his dark glasses. Silence. Someone watching that scene "from the side," for example, through the open window of the apartment in the house where Drama café is located on the ground floor, would watch it like a sequence from a movie by forgotten film auteur Jacques Tati.[3] One scene would be when a taxi stops unexpectedly in front of "our" café. "We," looking from below, sitting on the terrace, would hear music playing on the car radio. "Someone" at the window of their apartment, watching the scene like a "film sequence," would not hear the bang of the closing car door. They would watch the movements of unusually pretty Woman, to whom Taxi Driver, who had stayed in his car, was speaking right then. "We" on the café terrace would hear "have a nice time in our city," while the person at the window would have only a partial view of Woman, smiling, with pursed lips; would also see her wink at Taxi Driver.

"That woman" strutted, swaying her hips.

---

3. Jacques Tati (Tatischeff, 1907–1982) was an actor, screenwriter and director. He created and interpreted the legendary figure of Mr. Hulot. He authored numerous "celebrated comedies," was a "brilliant critic of civilization," an "artist with unique visual humor," "one of the greatest directors in the history of cinematography" . . . I had to think of him here. (Narrator)

At one moment Woman stopped, bent her leg at the knee, raised her heel, lowered her left hand to the raised foot, and with skillful fingers repositioned the leather strap that had fallen off her heel.

"Bravo," I thought.

"Well done," thought Dog.

"Sit with us," said Scott.

Woman accepted the invitation. She sat at our table. She made herself comfortable right away. She took off her sandals. Unbuttoned a button on her blouse; undid the zipper on her skirt; took off her sunglasses. She smiled.

"Mineral water?" said Dog.

"Cigarette?" I said.

Scott was engrossed with the iPad display in front of him. Woman took advantage of this to move close to him, purportedly to look at it as well, pressing her face against his.

They read the text on the screen for some time in silence: an excerpt of my text on the death of my friend Miodrag Vuković.

"Sad story," thought Woman and drew even closer to Scott.

"Story of my youth," I thought and gazed at Woman's beautiful legs.

Dragan Velikić[4]—at such moments I imagined him as the waiter—politely smiling at that group sitting at a table on Drama's terrace, bowing humbly. Seen from above, from the window of the apartment in the same building, it was easy to see that he said, "May I take your order?"

The wind played gently with the curls on Hairdresser's forehead. Suddenly it was a beautiful face. Green eyes. Like the leaves on a young cornstalk. Between her full lips—lipstick the color of oleander petals—her cigarette smoked like a signal of "eternal" reconciliation.

The toothpick in the corner of the mouth of Man at the entrance to the hardware store looked like the beak of a "fine" bird that had been sitting on the same branch for a long time. Man was actually reminiscent of a horse without a tail, rump, or hooves. He stood there, as though on the same spot, for a long time. And he really seemed "likeable."

Mother, with Child on the sidewalk across from Drama's terrace, looked like herself from another time. Was she considerably younger?

---

4. Dragan Velikić (1954). He has written numerous books, in particular *Via Pula, Danteov Trg, Islednik*. A friend. Here he is "a friend who is always here." (Narrator)

And Child, her little son, suddenly was a little girl. And she was not pulling a little car on a string behind her, but was playing hopscotch, hopping on one foot, by turns like a sparrow, ballerina, and rubber ball.

The bicycle that Cyclist was riding on the empty pavement was no longer a mountain bike or a racing bike, but was now a Chinese velocipede, without gears, without brakes under the handlebars, and with a bell that sounded in turn like the first bars of "When the Saints Go Marching In," the bells from a church belfry on Easter Sunday (for example), and a woman laughing hilariously, at an uneven beat.

Only Taxi Driver in his car, parked not far from Drama outdoor café, was the same as "before." His situation was different: he was not standing in front of the car, but was sitting behind the wheel. He did not speak to anyone, and was quiet. He did not keep his hand on the gear shift, but on the steering wheel. He drummed his fingers to the beat of the music from the radio (playing "When the Saints Go Marching In"). He nodded his head to the beat of the music.

At exactly 1600 hours, "Someone" at the window of the apartment in the building where Drama outdoor café was located on the "ground floor" closed the window. Before that they had pulled in the extended lower part of the blind. Then they lowered the roller blinds, and that made a loud noise. Waiter (Dragan Velikić), carrying a tray, stopped, frowned, and then continued walking backward toward the entrance to the café, clearly in a changed mood.

"I fuck your dog-mother," swore Dog (in the direction of the barking coming from a nearby street), but nevertheless wagging his tail happily several times.

Scott took Woman in his arms and kissed her tenderly on the forehead.

I surrendered to my thoughts: they were rather dark. As though dusk had fallen.

In the apartment on the second floor of the house where Drama outdoor café was located, all the windows were darkened. On the parquet in front of the window where Someone had been "a moment ago" looking out (down at the scene on the café's terrace), light stripes could be seen: the reflection of light passing through the thin spaces between the slats of the blinds that had not been completely lowered. Sonja—I now saw that she was the person who had stood at the window a moment ago, watched the scene on the café terrace, closed the window and lowered the blinds—was sitting in an armchair with her feet up, knees bent, heels tucked under her derriere, pensively staring blankly in the darkened room.

Above the window, where Someone had just been looking out, gulls, cormorants, ducks and swans were flying in a circle. Did one of the birds suddenly "slam" its body with all its force into the slats of the blinds?

Scott and Woman in the meantime had kissed loudly, passionately, and then again very gently. They sniffed each other. Their fingertips caressed the contours of their noses, ears, chins, cheeks, foreheads. They whispered sweet things to each other.

Dog was sleeping. He was dreaming of himself as a pet. By turns he was lying on the kitchen floor, standing next to a plateau in the garden and barking at length, running after children in a little park. He imagined himself as a horse. And periodically he felt like a chicken.

It is evening.

Night has fallen.

Is there any wind?

In the room where Sonja had recently sat (a moment ago Someone watching the scene on Drama café's terrace from the window), the circle of light from the lamp illuminates pages of the open book on the reader's knees—the novel *Train* (by Spasoje Stojić).

Sonja is visibly upset.

Konjović is reserved ("Who's this guy?")

Dog pricks up his ears inquisitively.

Woman and Scott, still embracing, wait impatiently for what is going to happen next to happen.

I look straight ahead.

Dragan (the waiter; now a doctor as well) nods his head obligingly. He spreads his arms. Smiles.

"Do something with your life! Any old thing. Make a clean break! Or are you going on like that until Judgment Day?" says the woman reading *Train* after a long silence, as though roused from a deep sleep. Now she is the woman with Child (Mother) (holding an umbrella).

I turn toward Cyclist on the pavement. He is still making figure eights, riding now with his arms crossed, sitting up straight, and smiling.

The Little Girl on the sidewalk (no longer a boy) is walking, or rather hopping, with her arms crossed. As though mimicking the cyclist. As though wanting to be someone else.

Mother, wearing sunglasses, sneaks a lascivious look at Woman and Scott at "our" table, and motions to the child to "get serious."

Late afternoon. The sun is setting. The last, red rays of dusk illuminate Hairdresser's eyes. Eyes now flash, reflections that offer themselves to be experienced and interpreted in "their own" way.

"Did six years have to pass to realize that the two of them are from different civilizations?"[5]

"Is there an underground clashing in every relationship?"

"Two dug-in armies, well-camouflaged, are resting on the eve of the final showdown."

"Did she suspect something in his look?"

"Is there a storehouse of thoughts somewhere in space?"

"Basements, shelters and family tombs."

"You are not just you, I am not just me."

"Those false versions of family mythology, invisible relatives, humid, moldy, isn't that terrible?"

"Do you love me?"

"Figure out her game. Night is falling. Wear out the beast with impudence."

"There seems to be some shifting between his legs."

"Naked and alone. Sincere and pure."[6]

---

5. Quotations from *Train* by Spasoje Stojić. Subsequent quotations are as well.

6. These were quotations from *Train* by Spasoje Stojić. No, no... the quotations are from the book *Montevideo* by Dragan Velekć, published in Banja Luka by Peter Kocic in 2015. It is a "duodrama"—a man and a woman speak about their lives, about the highs and lows of their relationship, during a drive to a distant destination. There is no book called *Train*, and the aforementioned Spasoje Stojić does not exist either.

His back to the scene with the ball of the reddened evening sun, now without sparkle and light, Man steps "deeper" into the hardware store, and when he is still several meters from the counter says, "A kilo of half-inch nails, a hammer, three, four kilos of rivets, and two double sheets of sandpaper."

Night in Bajina Bašta. Cool, quiet, fragrant, somehow quite festive. Empty little streets are darkened by the shadows of potted shrubs in front of the doors to closed houses. Dog only barks at the sporadic gusts of wind that move the branches of an apple tree and, as though suddenly awake, frightened to the core, ripe fruit falls onto the grassy ground bedewed by the freshness of the evening in which All Present are changed.

Mother from the sidewalk in front of Drama outdoor café is now (finally) Woman at "our" table. She is drinking beer and flirting with me, boasting about her real estate agency, and tenaciously trying to sell me a "lot" on the street above the central hydroelectric power plant. "I like afternoon television programs on health food," she says.

Boy from the sidewalk—a moment before holding his mother's hand and begging her to buy him ice cream—is now the bartender at Drama café who has come to the door, stood in the doorframe, and put one hand on her hip, with a cigarette inserted between the pretty, slender fingers of her other hand. "That apron looks nice on you," she remarked to the waitress (now Dragana), who smiled at her charmingly and a little bit impishly, in spite of being so busy with work (because now she was also a hospital emergency room doctor).

Cyclist, previously riding "with no hands," lost his balance, fell off his bicycle that then rolled over him, got up and, quite shaken, pant legs torn, started to swear. With every step, now pushing the twisted and scraped bike, he changed his appearance, bearing and identity. He was Poetess (Jelena Glogovac), and with the next step Soccer Player (Ilija Kecman). Then he was Art Historian (Zvonko Gazivoda) and Soccer Coach (Perica Kočić), and at one moment Actress (Žanka Č).

And just then, Man in a straw hat, after he left the hardware store carrying a bag with his newly purchased nails, rivets, sandpaper, hammer, pliers, and several wrenches, turned to look at her (actress Žanka). And just then, when he wanted to go up to her (actress Žanka), she turned back into the original Cyclist who was riding swiftly with no hands, still making figure eights. Man wearing a straw hat went back into the hardware store. And as he entered he said to the salesman: "I forgot a box of screws."

Hairdresser, still in the doorway, enters the beauty salon. Now she is bareheaded, having taken off the aviator's cap she wore as a pilot in an air force unit for several moments. "Is it possible?" she said, going up to the glass on the wide-open door. And . . .

And, just then I looked at Scott. He was sitting in the living room of his house on the prairie. And watching "on television" a movie about a pack of wolves that was getting closer to the cattle pen in front of his neighbor's house.

Dog, still at my feet, was now sitting and roaring with laughter; he was laughing at the jokes erratically told by Woman, right then a redheaded beauty, who had stopped associating with Scott long ago. She turned her attention to me. But she did not address me directly, rather through Dog—telling him, for example, "I don't know what Žarko thinks about it," or "Ask Žarko whether this joke about dinner in a restaurant in Manhattan bothers him"—because that "redheaded beauty" knew perfectly well that Dog and I were close. Ever since that day we met in Cologne. (I lived near the city pound.) (I heard him whining sadly.) (I took him home right away.) We not only became inseparable, but also understood each other perfectly.

Taxi Driver now sat on Drama's terrace. Alone at a table not far from ours. He did not look at all like a driver. He did not nod his head to the beat of the music that came from inside the café. He did not read a newspaper. A revolver was not in his jacket pocket either. He sat back in his chair, legs spread, and was now the director of the power plant in person (although at one point I thought "that might be musician Svetozar Burazor"). When Dragana (waitress) went up to him, I thought, "isn't that the head of the power supply company?" Even though the waitress was standing at the "regulation" distance from the table, I saw the two of them sitting together, smoking, engrossed in a conversation about something. Of course, Dog and I were with them too. The conversation was about the financial situation of our company. The revised budget for last year. And of course, about stock trends on the market. I saw myself as the head of our accounting department, but that could have been Svetozar Burazor too. (He came out of Evropa hotel). He sat at our table, and he looked as though he was waiting for a tram. "You can now cross Nemanjina Street," I heard in the distance. I heard myself giving a passionate explanation of current trends in some monetary institutions. I listened to my voice. I saw Dog nodding his head in agreement. I saw the head of the power supply company pouring mineral water into glasses: first Himself, then Me, then Dog, then Burazor, then Taxi Driver, then Himself again.

Now an airplane was flying across the sky above Bajina Bašta. "A jet plane," I said.

Dog nodded his head in agreement.

"Or was it a helicopter?" said Waitress. Dog nodded in agreement again.

When bomb explosions were heard from the direction of Ponikve airport, Dog yelped, crouched under the table, and huddled at my feet.

Director of the power plant (acting like Taxi Driver for several moments) said: "The axle on a tanker truck broke near the village of Beserovina and the vehicle overturned. Mazut poured out of the tank. The road between Perućac and Bašta is blocked. Livestock crossing the road there are rolling in the spilled heating oil. The Drina River is already polluted there. Villagers, who have already started firing up their brandy stills, think it is an act of sabotage. We will conduct an investigation. We will arrest suspects. Rescue teams have already set out from Užice."

I looked up into the sky. A swallow that had whizzed by "like a bullet" grazed Scott Abbott's head. Dog barked hoarsely. I petted him on the head, and said, feeling like the manager of a hotel: "Several things need to be highlighted with regard to tourism in our region."

When the waitress said, "Shall I bring some shots of juniper brandy?" I thought, "Couldn't I be the director of a cooperative brandy distillery as well?"

Dog, who again nodded his head pointedly in agreement, spurred me to additional thoughts on environmental protection, and that is when I perceived him as the president of Greenpeace for "this region," not just because he looked at me with a blank expression or because I seemed to hear him say, "I love whales and seals."

It is autumn. The leaves are turning yellow and falling. Warm wind spreads the fragrance of ripe fruit, pomace, and raw brandy.

A well-known group is sitting at joined tables in front of Drama café in the center of Bajina Bašta: Peter Handke, Zlatko B, Žarko Radaković, Scott Abbott, Slobo Rogić, Woman, Our Driver, and My Dog.

My Dog speaks first:

"Strong fumes from the first distillation of plum brandy that is being produced more this year than in past years make me constantly drunk and I feel like sleeping all day long."

"I feel that vehicles running on alcohol fuel are too slow for the needs of the local drivers," says Our Driver. He is drinking mineral water and chain-smoking cigarettes.

"Unlike Albanian tobacco, the local tobacco from Bajina Bašta is soft, silky, with a neutral smell, but heady," says Slobo Rogić. He is drinking beer. He is wearing a straw hat. He has a terrible cold.

Scott now has a short haircut. He is smoking a pipe. A glass of red wine and *The Book of Embraces* by Uruguayan author Eduardo Galeano are in front of him on the table. He is silent. Grinning. His eyes follow a wasp circling over a plate with slices of sheep's cheese, beef prosciutto, tomatoes, peppers, and green onions.

Peter Handke and Zlatko B. are now in the kitchen. They are preparing mushrooms for the grill. Waitress (Dragana) and Bartender (Sonja) are with them. And Cook (Stana) as well. They are sitting on stools around a table, cleaning the mushrooms we all picked in the environs of Bajina Bašta just a few hours ago. They cut off the rotten parts of the fungi with knives. They peel bruised spots. With knife tips they skillfully cut out pebbles that have pierced or stuck to the little caps. Peter's knife is a little Swiss knife with a red Bakelite handle. Zlatko's knife is a mini dagger by the French firm *Opinel*, with a curved and unusually pointed cutting edge. Bartender and Cook are using kitchen knives made in the *Zwilling* factory in Solingen in the Federal Republic of Germany. Cuttings are thrown onto old newspapers spread on the table. Some are pages of the sports section from Užička's daily *Vesti*. Some are pages from the local crime section of Valjevo's daily *Napred*. Some are from the culture section of Banja Luka's daily *Glas Srpske*.

"What is *Glas Srpske* doing in Bajina Bašta?" asks Scott, who is now standing at the entrance to the kitchen. Now he has long hair pulled back into a pigtail. He looks Chinese. He is looking at the group in the kitchen. Eating a banana. Grinning.

It is autumn.

Warm rain drenches the tables on Drama restaurant's outdoor seating. Waiter, Waitress, Cook, and Barman are standing in front of the covered entrance to the café. They are looking at the empty pavement. Telling jokes. Laughing.

I am sitting alone at a table. An enormous sunshade is above me and is now serving as an umbrella. I am reading the newspaper. I take sips of black coffee from the cup on the table. I laugh at something I read in the paper. At one point I pick my nose. Then my ears. Then I scratch the top of my head.

Waitress (Cica): "He's picking his ears."
Waiter (Ratko): "He has big ears."
Barman (Peca): "His nose is enormous."
Cook (Slavica): "Schnozzy."

Dog comes out of the restaurant. He has obviously come from the kitchen. He is carrying a bone in his muzzle. He comes to my table. Drops the bone at my feet. Starts to gnaw.

I look up at the top of the chestnut tree. A pigeon flies out of it. The sound of flapping wings. I burst out laughing. Dog jumps at the pigeon, then stops and watches the flight of the bird that has turned into a toy, an aircraft, cruising above the street, just as the crown of the chestnut tree has turned into a dense forest. Leaves and branches take on a bluish color.

A movie starts that is about My Friend Scott's and my vacation in a hotel on the edge of a rampant "exotic" forest, with birds of paradise, parrots, and humming birds flying in all directions.

We are sitting on the hotel terrace. I am reading a newspaper and sipping a strong sweet drink. I am laughing, probably at something I read in the paper. I massage the edge of my ears and my earlobes. Then I scratch the tip of my nose. Then I run my fingers through my hair.

Bartender (Zaza) is wearing a two-piece pink bathing suit. She is fixing us drinks.

Cook (Larry), in a white chef's uniform, a toque on his head, with comprehensive culinary skills, is standing over the grill and, through the smoke of the steaks being cooked, just for us, looks straight ahead blankly.

Waiter, wearing formal black trousers, a white shirt with a bow tie, black patent-leather shoes, bald, with a "refined" thin moustache, smiling, brings the first course—salad plates (bulgur, goat's cheese, chunks of papaya, chicory, rocket salad), with lots of pepper.

Bartender, very conventionally dressed, resembles a hotel guest, an "authoress," or "actress," or "psychologist," "or she might be the owner of a chain of optician stores in a European country," thinks a guest, who is My Friend Scott, sitting at "a table next to mine." He is smoking a cigar and leafing through his notebook in which he is writing about His Friend Žarko.

Scott is sitting with his legs crossed.

His face has a pensive expression.

His sky-blue eyes lie in the eye sockets such that they "see everything" "in front and behind," "upward and downward." Not just because of the drink that Scott "refills" generously, his eyes appear unfocused, but do not give the impression of absent-mindedness, rather they increase the stress of concentration of someone who is above all thinking. And those thoughts are "sharp," one would say, and hard, giving the impression that they precede every remark, feeling, and even perception. "There is a man who certainly has his own opinions," I think as I watch him leaf through his notebook, or write down words, or bring his glass to his lips, or rearrange his legs. "He does not interrupt his thoughts," I think.

I have known Scott Abbott for some forty years. We met during my stay in Tübingen. Was it in the cafeteria at the Faculty of Philology? Or in the library? Or in the student restaurant known as *Prinz Karl*? Regardless of where it was, our first meeting was the result of "preparations": the work of our common friend, John H. Smith, who studied with me at one time. (He wanted us to meet.). If it is even possible to say about me that I "studied." Because I might have been just auditing classes and some seminars. Because, really, I never had ambitions to study. Not even in the late 1960s and early 1970s in Belgrade. Not even in the early 1980s, after I finished my doctorate, when I was a university teaching assistant in the department of empirical culturology, working on a project researching tavern toasts in folk traditions in the Swabian Jura. We visited village taverns. *Schwarzloch*, *Two Aunts*, *Lambs*, *Den*, *Deviation*, *Checkpoint*, *Parterre*, *Bonavia*, *Bay of Pigs*, and *Chapel*: those are just some of the taverns in the towns of Honau, Tübingen, Wilflingen, Gammertingen, Hirsau, Kusterdingen, and Bad Urach. The work, which I did very conscientiously, did not interest me very much. I longed for new experiences. I always felt like an "artist" (sometimes like a "yodeler" too). I wanted above all an "artistic production facility." At once. Any kind. And anywhere. "Why?" I wonder to this day. What drove me to actions that were not immediately "purposeful"? Where did I get that impetus for artistic creation? Without solid ground under my feet, without any production space, without concrete action, without an "audience," without material grounds and proceeds? It is true that we are "born perhaps by accident,"[7] that "we have no impact"[8] on our prehistory and take no part in it, but at least now, when my personal history has already unfolded somewhat, when it has become "striking," at least to me, when it is determined by time, place, and some concrete action, I try to fathom the meaning of my history, the "background of everything," to draw closer to its conception, to reason it out, to feel, catch sight of at least a tiny part of what gave rise to it. To experience my personal story, even if "it" seems both impossible and improbable to me, and like something that never actually happened.

"I was born in Novi Sad, right, dear Scott?" thinking that I was talking to My Friend at the next table, although I had actually whispered those words and sent them, in my thoughts, to the secretary of the department of cultural affairs in the Vojvodina provincial government. I read the words from my notebook where I had "just" written a text about myself (or had I written about Scott?).

"It's sort of an autobiography," I said to Scott (and to that secretary back in the homeland). "It is also conceived as a diary," I continued somewhat louder, because My Friend (and the secretary back in the homeland) did not look up from his notebook (from his documents). "Because I write the date and place where the text is written on the side, in the margin," I continued.

Now Scott looked up.

He looked at me somewhat bleary-eyed. And I had the impression that he was not concentrating on me, but on the woman sitting at the bar (who I had imagined as the secretary of the provincial secretariat for culture). "As though he can see behind himself," I thought.

"What are you writing about?" I asked My Friend. Out of curiosity, and to break the silence.

"I'm writing your biography," replied Scott, and added: "And you?"

After shaking his glass energetically, making the ice cubes clink, I saw him take a sip of his drink that immediately, "presto," passed to the second state of matter, from the ice and liquid in the glass to the haziness of his pensive, bleary-eyed look.

"I wanted to ask you, where you were born," said Scott in a voice that sounded like red-hot metal drenched in icy water that had just been poured over an anvil. "In Zemun?" he asked, coughing a bit as

---

7. Dragan Velikić, talking to Milomir Marić on the television talk show *Ćirilica*, January 2013.

8. *Ibid.*

he spoke.

"I was born in Novi Sad," I said. "He was born in Novi Sad," I saw My Friend Scott Abbott write in his notebook.

"All I remember from that time is the smell of butane gas and vapors of instant coffee made in the kitchen of a basement apartment on a street by the Fish Market," I said.

Scott shook the drink in his glass and took a large swallow. He tilted his notebook with his left hand. He did not raise the pen in his right hand from a "point" on the paper. He stared bleary-eyed at the ashtray on the table and it seemed that he saw everything around him, upward and downward and behind him.

Scott Abbott saw me writing the text of my autobiography in my notebook. He saw my moving lips as I half-whispered what I was writing, at times before writing it, at times repeating what was written.

And I saw My Friend Scott Abbott focused on his notebook like someone kneeling before an altar, seeming to pray for our texts' good health, cheer, and long life.

That is also how the waiter seemed as he brought our drinks; he moved among the tables like a priest before the altar, swinging the tray like an icon lamp.

And the cook over the grill, seen through the steam of the sizzling steaks, eyelids lowered to protect his eyes from the unpleasant vapors, appeared like a believer the moment the priest ecstatically intoned, "In the name of the Father, the Son, and the Holy Ghost"—the sacred chant echoed by the waiter's "whiskey on the rocks," "Cuba Libre," and "a bit more ice."

So, I am sitting in a wicker chair.

The restaurant belonging to "this" garden, and the table I am sitting at, are located on an island in a distant sea.

I sit and write. I summon to memory pictures from past life. I arrange them as though leafing through a family album. I stop at a picture from time to time. And then look at it at length. My eyes sweep the surface of the photograph. If it is a portrait, I focus on the face of the protagonist. My gaze alights on the eyes. I move to the forehead. Then the ears. If there is a landscape, I move around on it as though it were real. I turn from one detail to another. Occasionally I pay closer attention. I enlarge it. Stare at it as at something unfamiliar. Why do I seek something else in everything I look at? I even distort what is most obvious and recognizable. I convert it into something distant and foreign. Why do I turn my life into something that is defined by neither time nor space? Why do I talk about what I experienced as though it never happened? Why do I tell stories at all?

It is evening.
Or rather, afternoon.
Scott Abbott is sitting in the garden of a hotel restaurant on an island in a distant sea writing the biography of someone whose life he has been following for several decades.

Scott knows that he is capable of writing his friend's biography. He also knows, however, that every life, including his friend's, is "unique" and "full of secrets." One cannot plunge into someone's life without using one's memories and subjective references. Scott believes that carefully researching data about the life of one's protagonist is not enough to produce an "objective" biography and history. "The story of someone who is a friend cannot be the job of a historian alone." "I am too close to my protagonist," Scott wrote in his notebook. "We have shared too much in the meantime," he wrote. "In the meantime, aren't the details of Žarko's story part of my biography too," he wrote. "Isn't what we shared during all these years of friendship etched in my memory," he wrote. "Then aren't my memories extremely important when writing about Žarko Radaković?" "Isn't my biography of Žarko Radaković at the same time, to say the least, an important chapter in my autobiography?"

Scott wrote these words in a notebook manufactured by a company that ten years ago took over the license to produce notebooks like those adventurist and travel writer Bruce Chatwin used on his travels.

If the notebook Scott was using to write his story was an immediately recognizable *Moleskine* "sketchbook," one might think "this writer sticks to certain practices when using writing accessories," but the writing implement Scott was using was an ordinary "mechanical pencil," the almost unrecognizable *Staedler* brand, that might have been *Koh-i-Noor*, or *Pelikan*, or *Bic*, or something similar. The pencil itself was considerably less conspicuous than how it was held: his fingers were pressed against the pencil so elegantly that they brought to mind other actions, not only writing, but, for example, cocking the trigger on a revolver, or jabbing a syringe into a patient's vein, or stirring sauce in a pan with a wooden spoon, or cutting meat on a plate with a knife, or gently drawing a forefinger over the skin on a lover's neck, or a tailor's proverbial, delicate fingering the fabric before sticking in marking pins, and at one moment I perceived Scott with his pencil as a carpenter preparing to hammer a large nail into a board on his workbench.

Looking closely at Scott as he wrote, I also saw everything behind the action taking place before me. Looking, for example, at the writer's pencil, I knew at once not only what that type of writing implement was called, but also the location of the store where it was bought.

So, I saw every detail in that writing scene. Also, I was watching with composure inspired by the tranquility of the absorbed writer and the writer was like that because I was watching him inconspicuously, unobtrusively, just what someone needed who wanted to be left alone, but also be noticed. I saw Scott's hand move across the surface of the paper. I saw letters written with neat penmanship; they followed each other like perforations made by a perfectly functioning device. And because that "machinery" reminded me of a printing shop, Scott's handwriting seemed "old-fashioned" to me. And because the letters in the manuscript were uniformly written, and because the lines of letters were so measured, and because the punctuation marks appeared so superior, and because the manuscript's lines of rows were always straight and the space between the rows was always the same, Scott's writing also seemed to me like stringing together abstract pictures, and like something resembling those rows of little pictures in Julije Knifer's notebooks, different, of course, but just to the extent that Julije differed from Scott, who had accepted Julije's language as his own, and who wrote that story about Me, Žarko Radaković, in Julije Knifer's language.

I looked at Julije's little pictures. And carefully read the story about me. (In fact I wrote a story about myself, and about Scott, at the same time.) And however much I was amazed by what was written, I admired him just as much. Because it seemed like something both familiar and unfamiliar to me. What was written (in fact, pictured) was to me both real and unreal, foreign and distant, someone else's and close. It appeared as both Word and Picture. I read. Observed. Dreamed.

2

Secret of the Absent Friend

Before Scott left, I went to the movies on Wednesday with Alex,[9] and now that Scott is no longer here, I go to the movies on Monday with Alex as well. "You know, Scott went to the movies with me on Monday, but now, since Scott has left town (Alex maintains that Scott just left town, and did not disappear) and no longer goes to the movies with me on Monday, why don't you go to the movies with me on Monday as well," Alex said to me after Scott disappeared (or "left town") (because ostensibly Scott "sent Alex a postcard from Farmington when he got there"). I said to Alex promptly, "Alright, we'll go to the movies on Monday too, since Scott has disappeared, even though you maintain he left town, and is, ostensibly, in Farmington." When Alex and I went to the movies on Wednesday, it was always the Odeon, and now, on Monday, we go to the Rex. And since Alex and I now go our separate ways right after the Monday show, and on Wednesday after the show we go to a restaurant, I figured that Alex and Scott had probably always split up quickly after the Monday show, unlike Alex and I on Wednesday, because after a show on

---

9. Alex Caldiero (1949), American avant-garde artist, poet, sonosopher, polyartist, performer. He is one of Scott Abbott's closest friends. "Alex is to me what Knifer is to you" were the words Scott used to introduce Alex Caldiero to me. Alex became a close friend right from when we first met.

103

Wednesday Alex and I went to a restaurant. "Out of habit," said Alex, "I go straight home after the show on Monday, not like on Wednesday when by habit we, you and I, go to a restaurant after the show, because with Scott (on Monday) I always went straight home after the show, not like with you (on Wednesday) straight to a restaurant. Now that you go with me to the movies not only on Wednesday but on Monday too, since Scott has left town, I don't have to break my habit of going to the movies on both Monday and Wednesday," said Alex. "Alright," I said, "from now on I'll go to the movies with you on Wednesday and Monday, since Scott, you say, has left town and is, ostensibly, in Farmington, and it won't be hard for me, even though, for me, Scott is missing, and that is really quite hard for me," I said.

I wrote the account of Scott's disappearance while reading (as part of my investigation into Scott's disappearance) a little book (taken out of the box of books I intended to throw into the paper recycling bin[10]) by Austrian writer Thomas Bernhard, knowing that while Scott was studying he worked for him as an apprentice, and then briefly as a secretary. So, I wrote my account while reading Bernhard's novella. I read Bernhard's novella and wrote my account, infusing it with Bernhard's, considering that my investigation was possible only by writing, through narration.

So, I wrote and I read; or rather I read and I wrote. And I went to the movies, on Wednesday, and now on Monday too. And on Wednesday "after the show" I went to a restaurant.

I cannot maintain that as I read Bernhard and wrote, giving an account of and investigating my friend's disappearance, I felt free, unencumbered, without obstacles; I felt caught in the labyrinth of Bernhard's sentences that put up obstacles, I thought, not only for me, but for themselves as well, so they inevitably led astray. Both the sentences and I, and perhaps Bernhard himself (?), felt "claustrophobic."

I thought (reading and writing): "Couldn't my investigation, my account of Scott's disappearance, proceed 'more easily' if I read some other book?" Couldn't this happen by reading something perhaps "closer" to me, at least, I considered, a more "permeable" and "expedient" book?

The Narrator of the account (of Scott's disappearance) certainly could not "get to the bottom" "of the cheerful narration" (successful investigation) by reading, writing, narrating, investigating—without

---

10. As part of my squaring accounts with the books in my apartment, an undertaking that will not be discussed here. I'll save it for another time. (Narrator.)

inquisitively reaching for a book by a writer who would be, if not the "opponent," "counterpoint," and "adversary" of Thomas Bernhard, then at least "different," thus a "complement" and even "parallel to" and "compatible with" the author (T. Bernhard) whose text he was reading while he wrote the first paragraph of this part of the account.

And—look here—Narrator is already taking another little book from the shelf, *Three Essays*, by another author, needless to say Narrator's favorite storyteller, Peter Handke (that is why he let that little book spend some more time on the shelf and had not yet thrown it into the recycling box).

And he opened the book to page forty-five, where the title "appeared"—*Essay on the Jukebox*.

Narrator started reading the beginning of the story at once. He read. He read, therefore, the following:

Intending to make a start at last on a long-planned essay on the jukebox, he bought a ticket to Soria at the bus station in Burgos. The departure gates were in a roofed inner courtyard; that morning, when several buses were leaving at the same time for Madrid, Barcelona, and Bilbao, they had been thronged; now, in early afternoon, only the bus for Soria was parked there in the semicircle with a couple of passengers, presumably traveling alone, its baggage compartment open and almost empty. When he turned over his suitcase to the driver—or was it the conductor?—standing outside, the man said "Soria!" and touched him lightly on the shoulder. The traveler wanted to take in a bit more of the locale, and walked back and forth on the platform until the engine was started. The woman selling lottery tickets, who that morning had been working the crowd like a gypsy, was no longer to be seen in the deserted station. He pictured her having a meal somewhere near the indoor market of Burgos, on the table a glass of dark-red wine and the bundle of tickets for the Christmas lottery. On the asphalt of the platform was a large sooty spot....[11]

Narrator, or reader, or writer, or investigator, raised his eyes. And he read, copied what he read, wrote what he copied, investigated (the case of his missing friend), and wrote his account:

Intending to make a start at last on investigating the case of his missing friend and to write an account of it, at the newsstand of a station in Brooklyn Narrator bought a magazine on events in the world of entertainment and the latest volume of a detective series. The counters were crammed with daily newspapers, weeklies, magazines, pulp fiction, and thin paperback books; that morning, while neighboring stores in that part of the city were starting a new workday,

---

11. Translated by K. Winston.

the street had been thronged; now, in the early afternoon, only the newsstand was open and several travelers inside were leafing through men's magazines. When Narrator went up to the cash register with his items, intending to pay, the salesgirl, or was she just the cashier (?), pursed her lips, smiled charmingly and said kindly: "Excuse me, just a moment, please," then turned around and walked provocatively to the next room. "Hello, can you hear me? Scott, are you there?" could be heard, perhaps, through the slightly open door. As Narrator waited for the salesgirl or cashier (?) to return, he wanted to experience something else in that store, so he turned and joined the travelers at the counter with erotic magazines. He picked several things out of the pile of ransacked and scattered magazines: a magazine for lonely men, a magazine with "not for women" written on it, a brochure for direct contact with individuals interested in direct contact, *Playboy*, of course, *Coupé*, *Séparée*, something with the imposing title *Private*, and others. He could not get the salesgirl or cashier (?), (she had just spoken with Scott, isn't that what Narrator heard?), (and she had addressed him so kindly, isn't that how it seemed?), out of his mind. He imagined her in the next room, hand on her hip, a telephone receiver on her cheek. . . . The numbers on the cash register keys were faded, worn out from long use, almost invisible . . .

. . . just like the worn-out cap of my fountain pen, even a little cracked in one place, that I used to write this text.

For as long as I can remember, books have seemed to be musical scores that I listened (and listen) to as I wrote in order to enhance and direct my focus on the topic; so I put on earphones to further enjoy the investigation into my friend's disappearance as I read, wrote, narrated. And "now" as I read the book and write the account of my friend's disappearance, I can hear music: a selection of various CDs that I had "straightened up" and "sorted" recently, and recorded some on my player. These were the albums: *Arias for Senesino* (performed by Andreas Scholl and Accademia Bizantina), *At Your Service* (Morphine), *Blue Plate Special* (Will Bernard), *Combustication* (Medeski, Martin & Wood), *Dinner for Don Carlos* (Nicolas Simion), *Hand on the Torch* (Us3), *Live at Donte's Vol. 1* (Art Pepper), Lully's opera *Alceste* (perfomed by Le Concert des Nations, conducted by Jordi Savall), *Quarto Libro di Madrigali* by Gesualdo Da Venosa (performed by La Venexiana), *Muy Divertido* (Marc Ribot), *Together Through Life* (Bob Dylan). After long consultations with Alex, David, Anne, Lyn, Silvia, and Diane, friends who knew me and the missing Scott quite well and were excellent connoisseurs of music, this was music that I considered might be of special assistance in my undertakings, in my investigation through reading, writing, and narrating.

I stood next to the bookshelf and, with earphones in my ears, stared ahead. I was conducting an "experiment": I let my eyes, "guided" by specific music, stop at will on a book in which something might be written that was reminiscent of the missing Scott. The CD I was listening to right then—did I already say it (?)—was the album *Floratone*, by guitarist Bill Frisell, and the book that "caught" my eye and that I pulled off the shelf was—I said it already (!)—*Essay on the Jukebox* by Peter Handke. I was no longer certain whether it was Handke's prose or Frisell's music that induced me to write my "account about Scott." And since what I did was the result of an "experiment," my account was by no means "unconventional," just as neither Frisell's music nor Handke's book was "experimental." "My writing was not an essay," I thought, although the title of Handke's book (*Essay about the Jukebox*) might give rise to such a thought. I never experienced Handke's prose as the "result" of writing "experiments," nor did I ever listen to Frisell's music as "laboratory experimentation" with sound, not even when he played an out-of-tune guitar on the album *This Land* (given to me long ago by My Friend Scott Abbott). When a literary critic wrote about some of my books as "literary experiments," no matter how hard I tried, I was unable to perceive myself as a "scientist" working in a laboratory "experimenting with words" (I never considered Alex Caldiero, Scott's closest friend and now mine, as an experimental genius); furthermore, some sort of irritation came over me; I was really mad at that critic; but, in the end, I just mumbled to myself: "Did I ever live experimentally?" ("Never," Alex told me in a long, candid conversation; and I told him the same thing.)

For as long as I have viewed myself as a writer—and what else could I have been in life (?)—I have considered it my "duty" to write primarily about my personal experiences, about events around me, but not the way they really happened, rather how they could have been. Since I experienced the world not only by reading books, but above all through direct experience ("first-hand"), my books, of course, always treated the "directly experienced" first, and only then what others had written. If my point of departure when I write is something "written," then—as can be seen in Scott's and my book *Repetitions*—I have the immediate, irresistible need to present "what I read" as "the writer's and my common reality." This was not only—I felt—Scott's and my need to re-experience Handke's Written, but also part of our mission—we felt—to give meaning to Reading with a new perception of reality as presented in the Written and to transfer these experiences into something newly written, now ours.

Wandering the border zone between reading and writing, above all between life and art, became the fundamental factor of my literary existence. Even the "nonliterary work" that was "my livelihood," i.e. functioning "in" society, became one of my key literary repertoires, providing "models" for future or current writing ("on the spot"). What reading was for someone else. (Indeed, it never stopped being part of the "foundation," "dictionary," "repertoire," and even "strategy" of my writing). Ever since Scott and I set out on the "adventure" of writing our books, often working along with music from a radio or sound system, the "logic" of writing as conveying "experiences" in text became clearer: the perception of writing as wandering on the border between experiencing the world directly or artificially, even if it meant "inventing," ostensibly, "one's accounts," here I could have, at least it seemed to me now, laid it out even more convincingly (at least to me). Because: we wrote while experiencing our surroundings directly; and we listened to music, read books, talked about them, and cogitated, in preparation for writing. Well now, if someone wants to call "this" that I'm writing now the account of my missing friend, my coauthor, Scott, or an account of listening to Bill Frisell's music, or an account of reading Handke, an "experiment," they can suit themselves. Giving names to things, defining or "labeling" what one has experienced—these have always been legitimate and even inevitable methods of understanding the world. When someone asks me inquisitively what I'm currently doing, haven't I most often replied: "Scott and I are experimenting, writing together 'four-handedly,' renewing ourselves, changing our state of affairs. And, actually, even when we are not writing but just experiencing something, we are preparing to write, even at the price of interrupting everything 'else,' as in the case of experiencing this disappearance of My Friend, a disappearance that might be real and invented."

So, I was reading Handke's story about the jukebox, writing my story about the disappearance of My Friend Scott while listening to Bill Frisell's *Floratone*. I almost forgot to say that in the past two decades that musician has been extremely "important" to Scott and me. In the early 1990s, Frisell had somehow "marked" Scott's and my stay together in Cologne. Just a few days after arriving in the city, Scott and I, independent of each other, attended a concert in the *Stadtgarten* cultural center by saxophonist John Zorn, and Frisell was part of the band at the time. I must admit that at the time I was not keeping track of events on the world jazz scene. Scott was. He lived and worked with many of the doyens of modern music, and for a time even collaborated with Thomas Bernhard, a brilliant connoisseur of all sorts of music from our time. I, however, was lagging behind. Living for a time in Tübingen (a music province?), I had gone to concerts here and there, more or less randomly; that is how I saw *Lounge Lizards* live; "thought 'this is it!'"; this "stage of jazz evolution" was the height of what I knew at the time; although, I really liked that kind of music.

I can still remember listening to *Big Heart* with Scott (he was visiting me in Tübingen); we were sitting at the table in the living room of my apartment on Hackersteigle Street; it was a typical "Tübingen" day: fresh, diaphanous air, the sun's thin, milky rays breaking through the branches of a white pine in front of the window onto the Österberg that "passed" like an isthmus through the middle of the town north of the Neckar River and divided it into two firmly structured "halves," both with a view of the meadows and clumps of trees on the "boundary" hill. "Doesn't this hill in front of us look like a whale's back?" I asked; Scott nodded his head emphatically, but soon repeated the movement, so I realized that nodding his head was not really communicating with me, rather "answering" the rhythm of the music we were listening to. "Let's have a cigarette," he said; and several moments later my forefinger and middle finger were holding a cigarette between my lips, right under my nose, while Scott had a cigarette in the corner of his mouth, holding it with his thumb and forefinger; "You look like Humphrey Bogart," I said; "You look like Jean-Paul Belmondo," said Scott; the number "Fat House" kept us in some sort of "delicate balance": its intensity raised the "pressure" and "revived" everything in the room, even the plants in pots on the windows, making the leaves vibrate to the rhythm that translated into an all-encompassing "harmony," while we felt perfect peace inside, and appeared to ourselves as demigods, time heroes, but without any pretensions to something superhuman: "We are not beautiful men," said Scott while we listened to the song "It Could Have Been Very Very Beautiful; "But that really beautifies us," I said, and put the record player needle on the number "The Punch and Judy Tango"; Scott was reclining on the couch like an Egyptian pharaoh and looking at me through clouds of cigarette smoke that were dispersing slowly, almost imperceptibly; I gazed through the leaves of the houseplant on the windowsill like a demigod, at wisps of mist gathering above the hill and catching on the tops of isolated pines with flocks of sheep grazing around them (of the music we were listening to, only cymbals reached my awareness, but I heard them as crunching sheep's teeth); "Could you be Hölderlin?" asked Scott, after I put the record player needle back to the beginning of "Hair Street"; the day before Scott had ritually walked from (his) Ireland (the land of his ancestors) to Hölderlin's tomb in Tübingen; Scott was an aficionado (and teacher) of Hölderlin's poetry; two days later he took the train to Gmunden, where work with Thomas Bernhard awaited him (on one of Bernhard's as yet unpublished texts); so, he was on vacation and visiting me in Tübingen; he was looking for "motivation", seeking "powerful experiences," getting ready to Write. I put the record player needle on the beginning of "They Were Insane," drawing attention to the band's guitarist, Marc Ribot, young but already known far and wide; Ribot's "thumping" the guitar strings reverberated in me like an invitation to the distant future.

Whether it was because I knew that *Lounge Lizards* guitarist, Marc Ribot, sometimes performed in John Zorn's "formations" (Scott knew it too), or because of my "ordinary" wish to listen to music labeled at the time as "core avant-garde," I was all ears, listening to Scott's stories about the art scene somewhere else, particularly after his brief stay in Brooklyn, where he collaborated with artist Jonas Mekas for a while. So, well-informed by My Friend Scott, I went to a concert by Zorn's group *Naked City* in Cologne. It was just a few days after I had moved there from Tübingen. The effect of what I heard that evening in the *Stadtgarten* cultural center auditorium—excuse me for the conventional description—was "shocking." The stage "evoked" the "entrance to hell," even though there was "nothing special" on the stage. The thick layer of sawdust on the floor, illuminated by dark-purple light, looked like "devastated land" after the withdrawal of a tsunami. The "dirt" I felt under my tongue, between my teeth, under my nails and in my eyes (filled with tears the whole time), had neither smell nor taste. Everything before me was characterized by death. Even the knocked over speaker, "resting" in the middle of the stage, looked to me like a face-down human corpse, now facing a sidewalk where—under the upper part of the speaker (if it had been upright, where the high notes come from)—I, not knowing "why," caught sight of a puddle of blood that was "still" spreading farther, always farther, during the entire concert, and "kept on spreading." And not that far from the "head" of the speaker (corpse) on the "cement sidewalk" (in the sawdust) was the "electrical" distribution box that looked to me, without knowing "why," like a revolver. It was aimed at the "head" (top of the speaker) of the "Executed" (speaker).

Like salvos of "automatic guns" and "clattering" machine guns, music roared on the "open stage" (in a deserted, dark part of town). The *Batman* theme resounded in a "version" that I would now, after the fact, describe as "*noise rock* or *country-groove*." Suddenly, after "things got moving" (the concert began), "all sorts of things" came one after the other, as though injected into the musicians' bloodstream, "examples" of all possible "styles" of our music "at the time": *country, calypso, death metal, trash rock, B-movie soundtrack*, and so on; there was even cocktail lounge music. Yes, it was the music of Zorn's group *Naked City*. The concert was part of the "tour" during which *Naked City* presented their first album, of the same name, today an anthology from the last three decades of the last century. "Terrific!" I said to someone next to me in the audience, even though there was no way that person could hear me because of the loud music, but he sensed I had said something and quickly "replied." "Terrific!" he said, although I could not hear him because of the loud music, but I sensed him. ("Was My Friend Scott there somewhere too?") We listened to that unforgettable concert by Zorn's group *Naked City*. The masterful saxophonist used every existing "theme and motif" from commercial and alternative music (!), said Scott after the concert, in a restaurant. The way he tore the themes, cut them into pieces, and glued them back together, I said later, in a restaurant, to Scott while we drank one beer after another. The way the parts of this and that unexpectedly "flashed," and then the next moment were suddenly swamped by an "avalanche" of completely different, seemingly incompatible "craziness," "with no end in sight"!

"John Zorn was and remains a technical collage master," I remember having read somewhere. "Isn't that true, to a certain extent, for Alex's art as well?" I thought at one point. "What Zorn produced in the late 1980s and early 1990s with *Naked City*, thus, before he 'discovered' his roots with the new group *Masada*, made Zorn the quintessential postmodern musician," said Scott. "We might say: John Zorn returned the true meaning to postmodernism," I said. It is indisputable that Zorn's "collages"—that also acted like video clips in which heterogeneous motifs followed each other at breakneck speed—"recycled" almost the entire music heritage of the twentieth century. This, however, is where Zorn's "eclecticism" was exhausted, because commercial music motifs, transferred to a completely different context, were no longer mere extracts, but had a critical attitude toward that seemingly "healthy" world of innocuous entertainment and exposed it as a progressively spreading disease. Zorn's collages, with interruptions intentionally breaking up wholes, with jump cuts "shattering" solid structures and every „form," in themselves still appeared like a perfect, homogeneous whole, in which we clearly noted, not only then, but "today" as well, more than two decades later, a metaphor for a civilization rapidly approaching the edge of the abyss.

I was no longer certain whether I had already read somewhere what I had "just" written, since "previously," in Tübingen, I had lived exclusively through reading, more precisely, "in what I read." But I could maintain with the greatest certainty that "now," "here," "in Cologne," I had to stop reading, and just write. I had to finally narrate. Exactly the same way that John Zorn (saxophone), Bill Frisell (guitar), Fred Frith (bass), Wayne Horvitz (keyboard), Joey Baron (drums), and Yamatsuka Eye (vocalist) did in the *Stadtgarten* cultural center auditorium that September evening in 1990. I too had a premonition of "evil" those years. I clearly "saw" that "approaching edge of the abyss." I had a premonition of "disaster." And I wanted to "narrate," to expose the disease that was spreading at breakneck speed.

The point here is not just Scott's and my experiences listening to John Zorn's music. I am not talking about reading Thomas Bernhard and Peter Handke's books here either. The point is above all about looking for "that" "key" "moment" when I "passed" from reading to writing.

Is it possible—or did I just imagine it later—that this took place at the *Naked City* concert when Scott Abbott and I bonded and became inseparable friends?

3

Accomplices (Witnesses)

Rastko

My name is Rastko. (For reasons known to just a few, they call me Vuk.)
 Actually, there was no real reason for me to work in the library.
 I should have done something else.
 Long before the events I will describe here, when I worked as a journalist, a profession I started right after I interrupted my studies—"I dropped out of school," I told my first wife, "I stopped going to classes and seminars because I had fallen in love"; "head over heels," said my aunt and classmates at the university—a woman named Marina Abramović (I wanted to become a journalist because of her) suggested that I "interview" her in unusual circumstances (for example, dropping from the sky under a parachute, or on the bottom of the sea, or in a volcano crater, or in a menagerie, or on a battlefield . . .).
 One variation in the series of those conversations was to be "realized" in a swimming pool not far from "Ljukovo" farm near Stara Pazova (in the former Yugoslavia). We traveled to that "location" from Belgrade (the capital of Yugoslavia at the time), specifically: from Zemun (suburb of the capital), by train to Stara Pazova (small town some fifty kilometers north of the capital), and then from the Pazova station to "Ljukovo" by horse-drawn cab. The driver, Vid Vlajković—a man of uncertain age, with an unusually "phonic" voice manifested primarily when he addressed the harness horses, a pair of thoroughbreds raised on the farm we were approaching on a dirt road between cornfields and long plots bristling with barley and wheat—

113

talked about his life: he was born in Šabac (a small town on the northwest of the eastern federal unit in the former Yugoslavia); as a child he moved to Bosnia, to a small town not far from Zavidovići (in the central federal unit of the former Yugoslavia); he was there when war broke out; he remembers his parents primarily for their misfortune, they disappeared when the city was bombed ("long, long after, they reappeared, but then it was too late"); he remembers spending time in a prisoner-of-war camp; he was tortured, they extracted and "repaired" his teeth through an opening in his cheek; he came of age at the end of the war; he tramped all around the demolished country; he tended livestock, unloaded manure, hauled sacks of flour in a mill in Surčin, help lay the Šamac/Sarajevo railroad line, worked as a pigskin tanner, a water diviner, slaughtered livestock, cleaned yards, was an assistant in a slaughterhouse, helped out in a blacksmith's shop, in pens and stalls, worked as a corn picker, until he settled down on the "Ljukovo" farm where he got his current job as horse and buggy driver. In answer to my question, "Do you like your job?" he remained silent. In answer to my question, "How much do you make?" he shouted at the horses and they started up a slow trot. In answer to my question, "Are you happy?" he laughed. It was only when I asked, "What time is it?" not addressing him personally, just in general, that he answered me directly, first raising his eyes to the sun, "Somewhere around four p.m."

Norbert Arns: About Four, Installation, Leverkusen 2001. (Photo: N. Arns)

We reached "Ljukovo" farm around 1700. I remember the sound of carriage wheels rolling along the gravel lane between the boxwood hedges. And our footsteps on the path in front of the entrance to "Ljukovo" villa resound even today as the stamping of horse hooves just before stopping next to the southern front of the building. And I still hear today the driver's shout, a ringing baritone, as the chanting of a priest. I saw Marina—a woman in her early twenties at the time and already of an indeterminate age, already with mature ideas, mysterious behavior, and more unusual than pretty—as a young mare.

First view from the terrace on the southern front of "Ljukovo" villa: to the right, in the western section of the park, a rose garden. Between the bordering bushes: birds with that primordial "primitive" shuddering, hopping and moving from one place to another. Swarms of insects set against the clear afternoon sky, magnified, like birds on a collective takeoff. Why did Marina Abramović's eyebrows appear to me like caterpillars that early evening? Why did her pubic hair (one night, in a dream) seem like a clump of moss on the roof of a building in the shade of a walnut tree? During the evening, outside under the sycamore in "full" leaf, I gazed at the puckers of the "calico" "summer" dress between the thighs of the woman I had fallen in love with "at first sight" and was ready to change my life, and even identity, for her. And in the semi-darkness I noted a stag beetle flying above Marina's head. I also saw a hedgehog crossing the path. And I heard an owl call. Above all, horses neighing in the distant stable. And barking dogs calling out to each other, sometimes loudly, wildly, then more quietly, then infrequently, then frequently, individually, then several together, sometimes having long "conversations," sometimes "discussing," even-tempered, and then they would burst into quarrels that heated up and became shouting, roaring, bellowing, and thunderous swearing. Oh, yes, in the middle of the night, looking out the window of my room (or did I only dream it), I saw Marina outside, disheveled, with blades of straw in her hair, in a wrinkled dress, looking too slight for the strong wind that suddenly came up from the west; neighing horses (and whinnying donkeys?) could be heard from the stable from behind which Marina had just appeared; pheasants, flying low over the swirling grass, streamed like projectiles into the bushes; roses, suddenly opening and then just as suddenly closing their petals, released powerful fragrances that spread above the vast "Ljukovo" estate in waves, in thick bands of mist, curtains of warm dust, drops of scented milky rain.

We started the interview around eleven o'clock, right after a drawn-out breakfast on the terrace in front of the entrance to "Ljukovo" villa. The swimming pool where we talked had not been filled with water for years (said Vid Vlajković the night before during our visit to the stable where he spent the night). The cement bottom of the pool, however, was not dry. Water had collected in uneven places when it rained. Insects could be seen on the surface of the little puddles. One of them, a horsefly, disproportionately large on the surface of the puddle, was unusually "beautiful." The colors of its body and iridescent wings were not only strong and clear, but also magnified by the reflections in the puddle in which I suddenly saw an airplane streak across the sky. The sound of the aircraft's engine was amplified. Even though it was a sports plane used for crop dusting, I heard its sound like the droning of a bomber. And when a whirlwind from the otherwise not so strong summer wind set in motion several blades of grass growing in the cracks of the pool's damaged cement walls, I felt fear, and thought "invasion." Those were moments when the surrounding "world" pressed in on me. I almost collapsed from the malaise that came over me when I saw the body of a dead bird right before me and a large number of ants devouring the remains. Another "unforgettable" image was the large bug, a beetle, turned "on its back" and "desperately" moving its legs. Even though I knew that all the adversities I saw before me were "in my head," primarily the product of my sensations, I felt uncomfortable the whole time. I almost felt to blame for everything, not only "here" in the swimming pool, but all around, not only what had happened, but what had yet to happen, not only "tomorrow," but much, much later, something that none of us, at least not Marina and I, ever suspected or dreamed.

That morning Marina was wearing "dirty-brown" athletic "shorts." Her "top" was a light-blue t-shirt. She had on *Adidas* sports shoes and light-blue knee socks. Early in the morning I had put on tight jeans (*Super Rifle* brand), with a black pullover over a blue-gray t-shirt. Around noon I stripped bare-chested. It was "really" hot in the swimming pool, I said at some point. And listened to Marina's answers to my questions; they seemed like the words of a teacher in a village elementary school: instructive, always with remove, as though spoken by someone who knew more than others. Noon. The strong sun illumines the bottom of the swimming pool in which Marina and I, without shadows, and yet like ghosts, call out questions and answers. At times we whisper quietly. At times we stumble over our words. At times we interrupt our words with a cough, sneeze, or silence. The conversation unfolds like a true account of us during "those years." And that was a time of general imprudence by a generation that grew up only physically while copying their parents' appearance. I, however, stayed on the sideline. My "adversity" was deeply rooted in the fact that I did not have any parents. Unlike Marina Abramović's parents who were reputable civil servants, my mother and father had been imprisoned on the penitentiary island of Goli Otok during my childhood. So I was unable to imitate anyone in anything. I was always alone. If I did have role models, who could only have been my aunt and my grandfather with whom I grew up, I did not take them seriously enough. I thought about my parents all the time while growing up. I knew nothing about them for a long time. My aunt and grandfather never mentioned them. Or did not tell the truth about them. Some sort of vacuum was formed very early in my attitude toward my origins. It was not, however, my aunt's and grandfather's conspiracy of silence that weighed me down with its secrets. If I suffered at all from my parents' absence, it was solely because I was unable to "parry" my classmates, my peers, in their frequent references to their parents. Whenever someone said, "My father did this and that," I had nothing to say about my father. I had no idea how my mother cooked, so there was no way I could tell my classmates anything about "Mama's cookies," or "Mama's Sunday soup," or "Mama's pudding." If I talked about "my aunt's oven-roasted pumpkin," someone would immediately remark, "My grandmother does that too," or, "I don't have an aunt," which I did not perceive as an advantage, rather a real defeat, because I seemed to hear that unspoken "but I have a mama," and that resonated so painfully that I withdrew into myself at once.

But already then, in childhood, one without parents, some sort of ability to look at the world differently was formed inside of me. In my protective cocoon, initiated by growing up without parents and by the shame of such a childhood, I became suspicious of everything that was collective. And everything around me took place "collectively." The entire community in which I was born and raised was declared a collective. Even the families everyone used as a point of reference.

I said that Marina and I were in a swimming pool. I also said that everything was taking place on the "Ljukovo" farm not far from the town of Inđija. Did I say that the conversation in the swimming pool proceeded like a game of squash in which we both fiercely hit the ball that periodically flew like a projectile from the deadliest weapon? Marina acted like a killer; and like the strictest parent raising her child (me?) with the firmest hand, preparing him (me) for every type of cataclysm, not only wars but eternity as well. Not only because our words echoed in the empty swimming pool, at one point I felt like I was in a church, and I saw Marina as a father baptizing his child, at the moment of offering thanks to God (for everything He would do for his child). Why did the father (Marina) speak in a tearful voice? Did I note a hint of bitterness in her (his) eyes? In answer to my question,

"Why did you get married?" she hit the ball so powerfully that I saw "stars" "in the middle of the day." At one point she knelt on the bottom and turned her face toward the swimming pool wall. "Mama," I whispered, or only thought. In answer to my question, "Who was the first man in your life?" she ran toward me, and I, who have always avoided conflicts, felt at that moment like a local politician right after giving a speech in a local factory, who then went to a nearby restaurant, accompanied by the factory managers, where I would (later) fill up on alcohol. Marina sat on the bottom of the pool in the "lotus" position, "several times" looking piously at the sky. Rustling branches in the orchard around the pool could be heard. The sky was not only clear, but clean as well. A good part of our conversation seemed to me like gymnastic exercises, each doing their own. Marina and I were not a harmonious couple. Not even that "first wedding night" on Makedonska Street in Belgrade. Not even on the music academy students' collective excursion to Košutnjak. Belgrade for me was always a "confined world" where I was constantly irritated by blinking, broken lights on advertising signs. In answer to my question, "So, what is the human body to you?" she turned her face toward the edge of the pool. Vid Vlajković was sitting there, calmly smoking a cigarette. At that moment, not only did I hear Marina's words as a "warning," but I also made a decision that would disconnect me from everything I had previously wished for. The sun, now at its zenith, shone down with full force on all the land and all the beings on "Ljukovo" farm that noon. Since they were utterly distinct, without shadows, without features, and lifeless, I saw them as prototypes of "everything in the world." I remember that after the interview in the swimming pool on "Ljukovo" farm, I left "speechless," "alone," and "for good."

I met Žarko Radaković thirty years later. Although, according to some information, we met earlier: ostensibly, at the very time I was "having an affair" with Marina Abramović. Žarko was involved with Dubravka Gojković, whom I knew quite well, we were coworkers, both at the local daytime radio. I was on the editorial staff of the amusement-comedy program, while Dubravka was, already then, "early," editor of one of the "sections" of the education and culture program. I worked as a "freelancer," and periodically collaborated with Dubravka's program. "That winter," in the middle of all the work for the *Saturday Night* show prepared by Vlada Jokić, Ranko Divjak, Nebojša Janković, Zoran Jerković, Branislav Surutka, and me,

Accomplices (Witnesses)

Dubravka asked me to do a report for her program on a group of Belgrade poets appearing at a celebration at the ski center on Kopaonik (in the center of the eastern federal unit of former Yugoslavia). It was around New Year's. The military hotel on Kopaonik was packed with guests. I had traveled to the event (in our station's Jeep) after calling the hotel reception, a junior officer of the JNA (Yugoslav People's Army), a certain (Vlasta) Bosiljčić, who had "rattled off" on the phone, "Just come here, Vuksanović, and we'll see, we'll find a place for you," but the "situation" in the hotel and all the surrounding "annexes" was such that it was immediately clear to me that finding a place to spend New Year's night on Kopaonik would certainly "not be easy." First they wanted to give me the bed of a soldier on leave, in the nearby barracks, in a room with fifty beds. I had not done my military service, having received a certificate from the medical board saying I was unreliable, inclined to depression, rejecting all authority, and even violent, so spending the night in the barracks was "out of the question." My curiosity was sparked by the proposal of the duty officer, warrant officer (Radoman) Labus (that is how he introduced himself), who was making the rounds of the army duty services just as I was talking to the duty receptionist at the hotel. Labus said, "There is a place in the dog trainers' dormitory." I, who grew up with a pet dog, loved animals more than anything, and I thought, and said to the officer, "Why not." But I was so upset when we reached the part of the barracks with the dogs (German shepherds), owing to the animals' state at that moment—they were howling before their evening feeding—that I, oversensitive to their brutal treatment, thought, but did not say it to the officers right away, "I can't spend the night here." I "temporarily" (I thought) put my things on the empty and made-up bed in the dog trainers' dormitory, and with a *Nagra* tape recorder on my shoulder (too expensive to leave it with my other things) headed for the hotel, a hundred meters away in the direction of the ski runs. Dubravka was waiting for me there with information about the upcoming program of the hotel's New Year's show, where the Belgrade poets would appear and I would report on them for *Radio 505*, where Dubravka worked.

Dubravka immediately proposed that I spend the night in her room, even though she was there on a short vacation with her lover, Žarko Radaković. I refused at first, but she insisted. "Why should you suffer in a puppy house," she said, "we'll make do for one night, there's an empty bed in our room," she said. After a brief hesitation,

I accepted Dubravka's proposal, promising that I would enter the room late, very discreetly, get into bed, and leave the room just as discreetly early in the morning. I agreed to Dubravka's proposal because I thought it was "friendly." "Great girl," I thought, and said it later to Žarko Radaković. Although I was always reserved toward her. Introverted. Never showing the passion and imagination of a lustful male. Perhaps her close relationship with her family was what stopped me from openly showing her all sides of myself. I had no parents, while Dubravka was always surrounded by close family members, not just a few distant relatives. Perhaps that is why I could not perceive her as a woman. In the best of cases, I felt her presence as the proximity of a mother. And she showed "maternal feelings" toward me. She was always "warm." Caring. Protective. Like a parent. Next to her, I felt like a child. Such was the feeling that came over me that night on Kopaonik, in the bedroom with Dubravka Gojković and Žarko Radaković. Dubrakva, in a nightgown, moving languidly from the bed to the bathroom door, seemed like "my mother," not only in the dark. All I remember about Žarko, in bed, covered with a heavy quilt up to his chin, never getting up a single time during the night, was his loud snoring. And that increased my feeling of being an insecure child in a family that had no chance to survive. Early in the morning, while they, Dubravka and Žarko, slept like hibernating bears, and as I dressed and packed my suitcase soundlessly, I felt like a lecherous son leaving his family home forever.

In the early 1990s, I met Žarko Radaković again, more precisely in 1991. That is when I moved to Germany. Žarko had already been living in that country for a very long time, long not only from my perspective. In some situations, he acted like a German. He did not socialize much with his "fellow countrymen" either. We were all employed together (in the archive of a media house, "in the library"), but Žarko always seemed on his own. As though he was not there when we had conversations in our collective. On the other hand, he was efficient at work. And he always got along perfectly, regardless of the circumstances, in an environment that was new to both him and me. He too had just moved to "this town." He was hired "here" a year before I was. Before that he lived in another city, but in the same country. In the meantime, the language of the people in the country where we "all" happened to be became "his." I, however, in the beginning used other languages to get along in this foreign city. I mostly hung out with fellow countrymen. And there were a lot of them in those 1990s. Because it was a time of emigration. The country where we were all born and raised was on the brink of civil war and disintegration. The upheavals that led to such "radical," "difficult," changes were so powerful that they triggered tall, destructive waves— on the surface of what had previously been such a peaceful, almost "swampy land" that many (not everyone!) considered "our country" all the years we were growing up—and destroyed everything that had been vital until then, meaningful until then, and drove everything to ruin, in the best of cases sending it somewhere else where the meaning of that once however small meaningful burden changed. If, for example, before "this" storm a boat "there" in that peaceful, warm sea, was reliable, modestly equipped, certainly a comfortable "boat," "here," after that terrible bad weather, thus, after the shipwreck, it was just a wreck, most often a shell of what it had once been, and what was left of it was either recycled or modified, as quickly as possible, into something quite different, for example an underwater "cage" to catch fish to be eaten in a hotel on the shore of a cold lake, or softwood flooring in an expensive apartment in the former port authority building, or spiral stairs joining two floors in a recently remodeled department store in the city center. If one of us, for example, "there" in our former country, had been a secondary school chemistry teacher by profession, now, after being forced to move to another country, because the country in which they previously worked so diligently no longer existed and war was raging in what remained of it, thus "here," in the other country, now those persons were forced to clean other people's apartments, or wash dishes in restaurant kitchens, or guard public garages at night, or incinerate garbage at the city dump. We also, "here" ("abroad"), indeed "happily" employed, unlike the many unemployed, always did something quite different from what we had done in our former country. A doctor of physics, otherwise a party official in the former country, now arranged books on bookshelves. A former ballerina in the national theater, "here" made coffee for the bosses. A chemist in a state-run enterprise "now" worked as a typist. A chauffeur in a ministry of the former country, "here" was a project coordinator. I was a journalist "there," a "specialist" for foreign policy, "here" I used "scissors" to cut out articles identified by "our boy scout" Nenad Lisicki, who "there" in our former country had been deputy director of an institute for social affairs, and now, after reading the newspaper article headings and photocopying the articles, sent them unread to one of our "editors," most often Velizar Mihajlović, in the former country a state security service agent, who read and "selected" them. What did Žarko Radaković do in our former country? No one knew. Željka, a former opera singer, now one of the three secretaries of our department head, Konrad Fuhrmann, heard that Žarko had once been in a relationship with Dubravka. Our chauffeur, Jelenko, once a cameraman at the state television station, was friends with Žarko's brother Miloje; if he knew anything about Žarko's past, it was only what he heard from Miloje, therefore, most often some detail from their family life, most often an event from early childhood. Živana the cleaning lady, otherwise a trained doctor, internal medicine, remembered that Žarko "at one time" went to the office of her colleague, gynecologist Đorđe Mišljenović, but never knew why.

I was attracted by Žarko Radaković's mysterious past. It "overlapped" with the "blank spots" of my former life. Because I too mainly kept silent about what was not "normal" in my childhood, turning "all of it" into a secret. I was impressed by Žarko's enigmatic smile at the question, "What did you do in the 1970s in Belgrade?" or his "mysteriously" raised eyebrows when asked, "What did you do in the 1980s in Tübingen?" or his inexplicably nodding head at the question, "What did you do after work yesterday?"

("One afternoon, after leaving the archive building where we worked somewhat earlier than usual, I invited Žarko to "have a beer" in a nearby pub. It was summer. A wave of unbearable heat. We sat in the garden in the shade of a densely leafed chestnut tree. We sat mostly in silence, gazing at the faces of the other guests, resting our eyes from the strain of reading "mandatory literature" at work. We appeared so calm that no one even suspected the violence and brutality we had shown at work just a few hours before, reacting to what was written in various articles about the disintegration of the country and the war raging there" . . .)

Danka

My name is Danka. I am not married. So, I don't have a "normal" family life. And I don't feel any "fetters" or "responsibility" toward anything. I am free. If I want to be close to someone, it certainly does not have to be a man. My sex life is not determined by gender. "Communication" is what "it" is all about, as far as I am concerned. And it's not just about exchanging information. Finally, I don't have a job just to earn money. Actually, I don't want to belong anywhere. Although

Accomplices (Witnesses)

I am always in a crowd. I'm not afraid of solitude. In a crowd I try to find meaning for myself. And what I am, exists in advance. And what I am can't change just like that. I'm not interested in anyone else. Communication is aimed at confirming what I am. And what I am is what I was. I don't think about the future. In general, what I think does not have much scope. Duration has value exclusively as a grid on which there are signs of decay. That is why I do not perceive love as an idea. I perceive a man, or a woman, as a body. I have never been able to love anyone. I said that to Žarko Radaković, one afternoon "after we had left work" "earlier," and after we had sat in a nearby pub. I saw him avert his eyes. Not once did he show what he might have been thinking. I was attracted primarily by his body. The fact that he always resisted my physical proximity, from the moment I was hired to work in the media house archive, excited me. That afternoon, when I was masturbating in the bathroom imagining his hand on me, and just then he rang my apartment doorbell, I wanted to surrender to him. While he was talking about Cecilia Bartoli's latest concert, I imagined him naked. He was sitting in the armchair and I saw him standing up. As he stood in front of the window, I imagined him lying on the bed. Under the fabric of his bright green socks, I saw the shiny skin of his ankle. I imagined a hole in the fabric with his big toe poking through it. I felt the roughness on the knob of his heel. It smelled of manure. I have not even forgotten the smooth surface of the slightly displaced floorboard with the sole of Žarko's shoe on top of it. Through the noise of traffic on the street came the squeal of automobile brakes. Žarko's stare cut the glass on the surface of the television screen. Why, in those moments, did I feel his hand striking me in the stomach? Why didn't it hurt? I saw Nana, Marijana, Regina, and Giselle naked, not only on the television screen: they were holding their hands over each other's vaginas. Pubic hairs resembled the wires in metal sponges to scrape burned food off the bottom of pans. Žarko just laughed when I told him that my ex (third) husband slapped me when I told him that the hair in my unshaven armpits excited him because it reminded him of pubic hairs above the vagina. My second husband was African. My first husband was English. Žarko was the only man who did not try to seduce me. He never commented on my lust. Even that night we spent standing in the kitchen in my apartment, he did nothing to show that he considered me a "woman." So why did I really feel like a "woman" before him? And that hot summer afternoon when he appeared at the door to my apartment with freshly bought

123

CDs of alto Andreas Scholl, I immediately put on house slippers. Or did I only imagine it as I sat in the armchair in front of the television broadcasting an episode of a typical telenovela? I, who have never loved anyone, let no one but Žarko say to me "this," "there," "that," "nowhere," "nothing." He, however, was actually silent. He sat in the armchair in front of the television and looked at me in the reflection of the dark screen. His shoes—which he took off right away in the hall—lay one in the kitchen, the other in the bathroom. He looked at himself in the mirror over the sink for a while. He combed his hair. A morning episode of "Dallas" was on television. I was lying on the sofa, reclining on my right side. My breasts, not only then, were not very small. My stomach, not only then, was muscular. My butt, not only then, was not only heavy and conspicuous, but overpowering. "You're a good cook," said Žarko at one point. "I'm a good cook," I thought. "You're a good cook," said Giselle, Regina, Marijana, and Nana in unison. "The male member does not have to be long," I said in a business conversation with my boss. I like the timbre of my voice. I like my back. I am fond of myself. I love myself. I don't love cats. I like horses. The man I lived with longest was deaf. The woman I persistently tried to seduce bolted one night without a trace. The curtain on my window has not been washed since I moved into "this" house. I had the best sex with a woman who imagined I was a dog. My most lustful man was wearing an oxygen mask. It is autumn. Two bicycles, with peeling paint on the fenders, broken spokes on the wheels, cut and tattered leather on the seats, deflated tires, leaning next to each other against a tree, resemble an old married couple. I feel, sometimes, like an empty freight train car. In the evening I feel like a mug for morning cappuccino. I like to hang out laundry. I don't like to go to the hairdresser's. I don't like to stand. I like my handbag.

Monique

My name is Monique (or, rather, Diane). I call myself Mo (or just Di). I actually do not express my opinion about anything (I most certainly have one, but it's no one's concern). I react to current events "from the gut" (or "from the chest") (or from my long, or short, fingers) (or only from my nails). I first set eyes on Scott Abbott more than three decades ago (or, rather, not that long ago). I was wearing a short navy-blue skirt (or a long brown dress made of rayon with splashes of dark green), black cotton, thickly woven socks (or bare legs, with a slit in the skirt on the side), and shoes with a low (or sandals with a high) heel. Scott was wearing light-blue jeans, faded from washing, with a tear on the pocket of the seat, through which the cover of his notebook could be seen. The fabric of his left front pocket, clearly faded, had a bump from the pencil in his pocket. I knew for sure that it really was a pencil, because Scott took it out of his pocket all the time, along with his notebook, and wrote down words with it. Once I saw him sitting in front of a window drawing what was in front of him. He was shading the outline of a building in the distance. It sounded like the straw mattress rustling on my ancestors' old bed in the village (or in the worn-out armchair on the stage of a theater I frequented). I was born, however, in a city. Or, rather, in a small town. I grew up in a global metropolis. And yet, far from city noise. On the day we met, Scott acted like someone from the heartland (of any country). That, however, was just at first glance. There was the scent of a city in his presence. Not only did he not press the issue, he tried in every possible way to hide it. Periodically he did it clumsily. (Periodically he acted like a caricature of himself). Perhaps he was oversensitive. (Periodically he was oversensitive). He went from one extreme to another. At that first meeting I saw something crazy in Scott's eyes. (I saw someone's need to "get under my skin." I saw someone's need to "get under my skin.") But the very next moment his eyes were mild, a bit far away. As though staring blankly. I clearly recognized myself in his face. (I clearly recognized myself in his face.) I saw the embodiment of my curiosity. Along with my desire to be alone. I did not deviate from my needs. I did not change my habits. Need I say that at ten in the morning I went to my coffee house for breakfast? Scott was there. We sat alone at the table. He spoke about himself vivaciously. He drew me into the sphere of his stories. He looked like the protagonist of his accounts. Every story started by underscoring the presence of lots of protagonists who replaced each other at times, appeared together at times, took leave of each other on the "open stage" at times like the scene of a mysterious event in which, however, the "place, time, and plot" of the account were unclear. The traits on Scott's face were like that too: at times highly in accord with each other, at times canceling each other. At one point Scott's face appeared completely colorless, like an empty piece of paper. When his eyes flashed convincingly, they radiated a strength that crept into every corner of the picture, slipped under every detail, entering into the pores of painted objects and beings, disappearing in the whirlwinds of thought expressed in our conversation at breakfast. I ate a roll with butter, and on it a slice of ham and cheese. Scott drank coffee and smoked a cigarette. His eyes followed every movement of my lips as I chewed. For a while he stared at my ears. In fact, even when I said something to him, he rarely looked me in the eyes, rather at my eyebrows. And I saw that with one brief look at my pupils, he had "recorded" my field of vision. I saw that he was particularly interested in the colors I perceived. And he didn't focus very long on a colored surface. Not once did his eyes "stagnate." They moved: left, right, up, down, forward, backward, back and forth. "His eyes played around." "They flew," simply, "above the scene of the picture": high, low. Zigzagging, performing acrobatics, upside down. Then they suddenly plunged to an indefinite place, but one quite definite and chosen by "him," the pilot in Scott's eyes. He cut into the surface of the view. Plowed it. And then suddenly he soared up high. I must say that I particularly liked Scott's gentle gazing at my eyelashes. I cannot omit the low-flying cruising around my pupils. He drew lines on the whites of my eyes. He gently touched my pupils. He composed the most varied and multicolored designs. He painted quite nicely around my field of vision. He drew stripes: thick, thin, broken, dark, light. Here and there he scribbled on my view as though on a sheet of paper. As though writing something down. And it was: at times nice handwriting ("penmanship"), at times nervous scrawling, at times real scribbling. And each time he went across the "paper of my field of vision" there was the proper flashing of his eyes. I retaliated by looking daggers at him. At times we pricked each other, scratched (with our eyes), at times slapped, beat each other, at times pushed and tripped each other. Then we fell into each other's arms, caressed each other tenderly, massaged each other intimately, and in the end we bathed together and dried each other with towels. It was a conversation in which nothing was left unsaid, in which everything was said. And after a conversation like that, going back to the office after breakfast, we were able to get down to work "most eagerly." And we worked without a break. Without a word. ("Only our breathing was heard in the dead silence"...)

Afterwords and Portraits

We

Alex Caldiero

Regarding We

for Scott & Žarko

WE: always WE: the two of us: W & E: together or not together,

it is the tether that keeps us a part of who each is without the other:

of what each knows about and thru the other: no doubt:

the repetitions and convolutions of events only serve to replicate

and further weave who we are: who we is: finally the hope

of becoming singular, grammatically, at least: yet not one:

never one: for one is the dimension of infinity no one can enter

and breathe to tell: yet we can dare and do tell: and here is proof:

here in words we share and shear until they are un-recognizable:

every place we have ever inhabited: every space we have ever

We

occupied: each is ever becoming a *sphere* we will and have and must
and should and never forget is ours: or else what good or use
can each be to each: *yous* see, we are always in the middle of what
is passing by or appearing approaching ahead: gone gone gone
paramita para object always gone and going: a sound we can
follow into silence more deafening than any sound: do you hear how
the cliché turns into a most profound truth?: a nearly found fact:
a nearly formed act: I read these words even as I write these words
behind me coming to the fore one by one: we are poles apart
on a concave globe mirror wherein darkness shifts with every breath
taken or not, but lived and spoken: who is the teller of futures?:
who is the rememberer of distant events?: we take turns: obvious
remedies suggest themselves: this reading written is an antedote
no healer will deny you: you who only know the half of it: every
page of a book is a diptych: a predicament no one alive can escape:
w one half of we: *e* the half we fully pronounce and are::

Nina Pops

Portraits

"Scott und Žarko" für Scott 15.4.2013   N. Pops

We

"Žarko i Scott" za Žarka 2013   N. Pops

About the Authors

Scott Abbott is the author of *Fictions of Freemasonry: Freemasonry and the German Novel* (1991), *Wild Rides & Wildflowers: Philosophy and Botany with Bikes* (with Sam Rushforth; 2014), *Immortal for Quite Some Time* (2016), *The Perfect Fence: Untangling the Meanings of Barbed Wire* (with Lyn Ellen Bennett; 2017), *Dwelling in the Promised Land as a Stranger* (2022), and three books with Žarko Radaković: *Repetitions* (2013), *Vampires & A Reasonable Dictionary* (2014), and *We: On Friendship* (2022). He translated Peter Handke's *A Journey to the Rivers: Justice for Serbia* (1997), Handke's play *Voyage by Dugout: the Play of the Film of the War* (2012), Handke's lengthy ode *To Duration* (2015), and the documentary film *Peter Handke: In the Woods, May Be Late* by Corinna Belz (translation for the subtitles; 2016). *On Standing: Variations on the Standing Metaphor* is his current project, tracing and analyzing the metaphor in works by Sophocles, Rilke, Heidegger, Bruegel, Bosch, Holbein, Dostoevsky, Faulkner, Morrison, Kleist, and Woolf. He blogs at "The Goalie's Anxiety" (https://thegoaliesanxiety.wordpress.com). Professor of Integrated Studies, Philosophy, and Humanities at Utah Valley University, he lives in Woodland Hills, Utah.

Žarko Radaković is the author of *Tübingen* (Belgrade, 1990), *Julije Knifer* (Belgrade, 1994; Zagreb, 2018), *Ponanvljanje / Repetitions* (with Scott Abbott; Belgrade, 1994; Brooklyn, 2013), *Emigracija /* Emigration (Belgrade, 1997), *Pogled /* The View (Belgrade, 2002), *Vampiri & Razumni rečnik / Vampires & A Reasonable Dictionary* (with Scott Abbott; Belgrade, 2008; Brooklyn, 2014), *Strah od Emigracije /* Fear of Emigration (Belgrade, 2010), *Era / A Story of Era Milivojević* (Belgrade, 2010), *Knjiga o muzici /* A Book about Music (with David Albahari; Belgrade, 2013), *Kafana /* Tavern (Novi Sad, 2016), *Krečenje /* Reparative Painting (Novi Sad, 2018); *Putovati* (Traveling, Novi Sad, 2021), *Knjiga o fotografiji* (A Book about Photography, with David Albahari, Belgrad 2021). He has translated twenty-seven of Peter Handke's books into Serbo-Croatian and has been traveling companion and translator for Handke during repeated trips to Serbia, Bosnia, Montenegro, and Kosovo. He collaborated on three performances with performance artist Slobodan Era Milivojević (1971, 1973, and 1974). His work with Serbian/German artist Nina Pops includes collaboration on a series of collages that feature Žarko's manuscript translations of Peter Handke's novel *The Loss of Images* and Pops' "translations" of the text into images. In conjunction with his *Book about Art*, he and Pops mounted a joint exhibition in Cologne: *Gegenüber / vis-à-vis* (2021). He edited an edition of the German literary magazine *Nachtcafé* on the theme of "walking" (1998/89), and an edition of the German literary magazine *Schreibheft* on "Literature from Serbia" (in collaboration with Peter Handke, 2008). He lives in Cologne, Germany.

Acknowledgements

Deb Thornton, Professor of English at Utah Valley University, and her students Jamie Lewis Holt, Elizabeth Berdan, Blake Branin, Janice Chorniak, Cheyanne Dye, McKinli Grover, Megan Petruka, Esther Rogers, Jade Watkin, Shaye White, and Candice Wilcox, edited and typeset this book. They did so joyfully and generously, lending rare spirit to the resulting text.

UVU colleague and friend Mark Olsen worked on several iterations of our book. The cover design, based on Scott Abbott's photo of clouds over Utah Valley, is his creation.

We are grateful to Andy Hoffman, publisher of Elik Press, for adding our book to a catalogue that includes Beat authors Allen Ginsberg, William S. Burroughs, Laurence Ferlinghetti, Carolyn Cassady (former wife of Neal Cassady), Gordon Ball, and Anne Waldman, along with fascinating books and chapbooks by Joel Long, Ken Brewer, Hector Ahumada, Melissa Bond, Michael McLane, Alex Caldiero, and Hoffman himself.

www.ingramcontent.com/pod-product-compliance
Lightning Source LLC
Chambersburg PA
CBHW050818090426
42737CB00021B/3432